Marketing:

THE MANAGEMENT WAY

ARNOLD K. WEINSTEIN, B.S.(Econ.) (Penn.), M.B.A. (Col.)

School of Business Administration
University of New South Wales

WEST PUBLISHING CORPORATION PTY LTD

1 Barrack Street, Sydney

1967

To Judy

Wholly set up and printed by Bridge Printery
Pty Ltd, 117 Reservoir Street, Sydney.

Registered in Australia for transmission through the post as a book.

DATE DUE

Marketing:

THE MANAGEMENT WAY

Table of Contents

95819

Preface

WHY does someone write another marketing management text? *Marketing: The Management Way* is written to serve several audiences that have been neglected in the marketing literature currently available. I have attempted to meet the needs of marketing executives who have had no formal training. I have also tried to satisfy the desire of the marketing student who wants a book that will synthesize the mass of data he is exposed to in his formal marketing education.

This book should provide the practising executive with a practical approach to his very difficult job. It should also be a valuable stimulant for discussion in marketing management training courses. The chapters of *Marketing: The Management Way* are short, hopefully clear and concise statements of the types of considerations to be made in solving marketing problems.

Much of the material presented in this book has been said before. Unfortunately, it has been said in many different places and in many, many words. I have attempted to present the thinking of leading teachers in marketing and I have kept these lessons as short as possible. Where others have covered an area exceptionally well, I have outlined their teachings and made as few changes as possible.

The chapters of this book do not solve any management problems. Rather they present a managerial approach to the solution of marketing problems. Within each chapter there is the underlying assumption that marketing management must and can be done in a professional manner.

In preparing a work of this type, one ends up owing thanks to a great many people. First, I would like to thank the members of the staff of the School of Business Administration, University of New South Wales, for their help and encouragement. Second, I would like to thank the secretarial staff of the School for their tremendous effort in deciphering my hieroglyphics and turning them into a finished manuscript. Finally, I would like to thank my wife, Judith, who bore the burden of proof-reading my manuscript and who must have felt herself orphaned by my writing habits.

January, 1967   A.K.W.

1

Scope and Nature of
Marketing Management

THE term marketing is not new to our vocabulary, but very few people will give the same answer when you ask, "What is marketing?" A housewife will tell you she does marketing when she shops for the family's food. The salesman is marketing when he calls on a customer. And the farmer does marketing when he brings his produce to market. These are all aspects of marketing, but they are only small parts of a much larger discipline.

The first academic definition of marketing to gain wide acceptance was that of the American Marketing Association. "The performance of business activities that direct the flow of goods and services from producer to consumer or user." Under critical contemporary analysis this definition breaks down. One is left with the feeling that this definition starts "marketing" with a completed product and ends it with delivery of the product to the consumer. The little we do know about marketing theory forces us to reject any definition that does not include the pre-production and post-delivery aspects of marketing management.

In a current and well-accepted elementary marketing text, marketing is defined as follows: "The performance of all activities necessary for ascertaining the needs and wants of markets, planning product availability, effecting transfers in ownership of products, providing for their physical distribution, and facilitating the entire marketing process".[1] If you wanted a functional task-oriented definition, Beckman's treatment

---

[1] Beckman and Davidson, *Marketing*, Ronald Press, New York, 7th Ed., 1965, p. 4.

1

would be satisfactory. How many of you would be happy if your doctor defined the practice of medicine in the same way. "Medicine is the practice of seeing patients, analyzing their problems, prescribing a cure and receiving payment." I think most of us would find a new doctor.

To my way of thinking, marketing is an organized system of behaviour that functions for the purpose of evaluating and facilitating the satisfaction of consumer needs. Many of you will be thinking that this is a very broad definition. It is meant to be exactly that. Only through a broad definition of marketing can management begin to understand the even more important "marketing concept".

Most marketing texts and discussions always assume the operating unit to be a business enterprise. It would not be wrong to assume the operating unit to be a government, church or social group. All that is necessary is a change of words from consumer to "public". This concept should become clear as you gain understanding of the need for consumer orientation.

The Marketing Concept

Before moving into a discussion of the marketing concept, let us take a look at two parallel changes in management philosophy that have led up to the concept. Earliest management in an industrial society has always been production oriented. Marketing was a peripheral problem in the same class as accounting. Marketing was necessary only to distribute productive capacity. The customer was assumed and no effort was made to satisfy his particular needs. Because customer demand usually outstripped productive capacity, this was a perfectly valid and operative management philosophy.

Along with production-oriented management, there tends to be a non-public orientation towards social responsibility. Management has as a basic philosophy the subordination of all activities to the direct effort of making increased profits. The primary interest is to serve the property interests of the corporate shareholders.

As customer demand and productive capacity come into a type of equilibrium, management is forced to rethink its marketing philosophy. Competition forces realization that production cannot be sold without an effective sales force. To be effective, management has to supply its sales force with ground support in the form of advertising, marketing research and sales training. This is still a production orientation. Customer importance is realized, but only as a means of disposing of corporate production. To differentiate this stage, we call it sales orientation.

With increased competition, especially in consumer goods, companies in the sales-oriented stage of development begin to have troubles. Rapid changes in consumer demands continually leave the organization in turmoil. Analysis of the trouble shows that these companies are trying to sell products that were successful in the past without making an effort to adapt to the changing consumer. In order to succeed, these companies must realize the critical importance of the customer.

As customer orientation becomes the accepted marketing philosophy, the entire corporate philosophy undergoes a subtle change. Modern corporate philosophy has as its aim long-term profits, along with a basic concern for those who have committed their property. The property being committed is the time and effort of employees, the community life that is dependent on the industry, the money of creditors and the property of suppliers, the time of customers and, of course, the investment of the shareholder.

Lazer and Kelly, in *Managerial Marketing: Perspectives and View Points,* list ten criteria that must be met to consider a firm as customer oriented.

"1. The company appreciates and understands the consumer's strategic position as a determinant of the firm's survival and growth. The entire marketing system is designed to serve consumer needs in companies operating under the marketing concept.

2. It is assumed that marketing activity which serves consumers' needs can be planned, and corporate destinies shaped to a large extent, by planned marketing efforts.

3. Short- and long-range planning of company activities on a continuing basis, and the development of consistent strategies and tactics resulting in an integrated system of marketing action, are seen as the key to marketing management's tasks.

4. Marketing and business research is utilized to arrive at more fact-founded decisions. Research, including a system of intelligence, is becoming indispensible in modern marketing planning and action.

5. The significant role of marketing intelligence in establishing corporate goals and targets is recognized. Market potentials, rather than production resources, become guides to corporate marketing action.

6. Intra- and inter-departmental implications of marketing decisions and actions of various organizational units are recognized and the integration of all marketing effort is sought.

3

7. Programmed process and product innovation is accepted as standard and necessary.
8. New product planning and development and their impact on company profits and position are recognized and emphasized in corporate policy.
9. A marketing focus is adopted to co-ordinate company effort and establish corporate and departmental objectives consistent with the firm's profit goals.
10. There is a continual reshaping of company products, services, and other activities to meet the demands and opportunities of the market place effectively."[2]

Marketing and Change

There is one basic problem common to all marketing administrators. What place does change play in an organization and how do you cope with change? While it may seem obvious to say every company must organize for change, it is the exceptional company that has a formalized programme to expedite change. Drucker has said the two basic functions of a business enterprise are marketing and innovation. It is the blending of these two functions that enables a company to meet an ever-changing customer structure.

It has been said that "the real challenge to marketing people is to firmly get hold of the idea that changing a business, finding it new sales, new customers, new markets, is even more important than operating it efficiently."[3] What the author is saying is that the need for creative innovation is far more important than wringing the last ounce of efficiency from a production system. Productive capacity is of little value if it can only produce unwanted goods and services. When looked at closely, one finds that successful companies fully understand the place and value of new products.

We may ask ourselves why new products are so important. The answer comes back to the persistent management problem; change. Ours is a society based on change. Cultural changes take place continuously. Technological change is taking place so quickly that computers must be used to keep libraries up to date. Political and economic changes are everyday experiences. Each of these changes has a profound effect on the consumer and on the producer.

In addition to these macro-environmental changes, there are

---

[2] Lazer and Kelly in *Marketing Strategy and Functions,* Prentice-Hall, New Jersey, 1965, pp 9-10

[3] Ibid., p. 9.

4

simple market place changes that create the need for new products. Shifts in customer purchases create direct changes in a company's sales. Changes in customers' manufacturing methods can be the cause of immediate product obsolescence. Customer moves will quickly remove a firm's only competitive advantage.

A single simple reality of marketing causes the greatest need for product innovation. When a product reaches maturity, the cost of increasing sales goes up much faster than the profits from any increased sales.

In industries subject to the pressure of market competition, there is a distinct product life cycle. During its life, a product usually passes through the following stages: pre-introduction, introduction, growth, maturity and decline. Each stage in the life cycle is typified by a unique sales-profit relationship.

"Pre-introduction" is that stage in a product's life when it receives approval for further study and moves through the development process. This stage would include all market and design research. It would include pilot runs or preliminary model building. The stage ends with final approval for manufacture or sale. The length of time a product stays in "pre-introduction" depends on three factors: the availability of technical data and trained personnel, proper definition of market requirements and lastly, the willingness of management to take risks. It is obvious that "pre-introduction" represents a relationship of all cost and zero revenue. The measurement of these costs should include estimates of opportunity cost, in addition to direct out-of-pocket expenses.

A product's market life begins with "introduction" to the consumer. "Introduction" is usually a high cost, low profit operation. Gaining consumer acceptance is an expensive procedure. Building a better mousetrap will not automatically bring profitable sales to your door. If a product is one of the forty to fifty per cent of new products that succeeds, introduction should lead to a very profitable "growth" phase.

The snowballing effect of product demand by opinion leaders and early innovators makes "growth" most profitable. During this period the firm holds a strong advantage over competition because of its being first with a new product. Competitive advantage is eventually eroded. New products, even if protected by patent, can be copied or improved upon. The high profits of the "growth" stage will tempt many new producers to compete directly or indirectly. Initially, this will have the effect of slowing sales and reducing profit.

As the total market for a new product stabilizes, it enters

5

the "maturity" phase. Competition will continue to enter the market until it is no longer profitable. In an effort to maintain market share, profits will decrease sharply. During "maturity", the small firms that jumped on the bandwagon during "growth" will slowly drop out of the race. A new level of operation will establish itself and continue until something happens to disturb the mature product.

The something referred to above will usually be a significant technological change making the mature product obsolete. Obsolescence will cause a rather abrupt drop in sales. Heavy capital losses can be incurred and, unless a firm has prepared for the change, obsolescence may cause bankruptcy.

At this point you may be saying that the product life cycle concept is very interesting, but what is its value? Stated simply, the phase of the life cycle should determine the amount of risk management takes with a product. Products in the "growth" stage may represent a need for building new plant capacity. The same product while in the "maturity" phase would hardly be considered as cause for increasing capacity. Phase of life cycle should also govern the amount of money spent on promotion to increase sales. The phase of the life cycle is therefore an important management consideration.

General factors to consider in determining a product's place in its life cycle are: profit, competition and customers. How profitable is the product today as compared with last year and the year before? Is competition non-existent, still coming on strong or dropping off? Are customers more demanding in areas of price, service, and special features?

Theodore Levitt, in his article "Marketing Myopia", outlines certain management misconceptions that have led otherwise dynamic companies to neglect new product development. Some managements claim that growth in sales is guaranteed by growth in population. On other occasions even more absurd sentiments are voiced. There is no substitute for our product. Reality shows that continued population growth is likely to stimulate the rapid changes in technology that make once firmly entrenched products fall into obsolescence.

The first step a company takes towards developing a proper attitude on new products is realizing that innovation must be managed. Innovations must be managed because managements have a tendency to grow anti-innovation and organizations tend to inhibit innovation.

It may seem strange to say management tends to become anti-innovation but the factors causing it are quite real. With the introduction of quantitative methods, management begins to want more certainty in forecasting the future. New products are by nature a very uncertain investment. Successful companies build up a background of knowledge and tradition that tends to inhibit innovation and free thinking. Increased automation has an inhibiting influence on innovation as it makes great demands for a smooth-running organization. Finally, the temptation to make maximum profits in the current operating period stifles long-range product planning and innovation.

What can the individual manager do to overcome this backward inertia of the organization? First, he must believe in the value of innovation. He must ask his subordinates to innovate and introduce change. Innovation must be a matter of continuous concern and not a passing fancy. The manager must encourage critical review of past, present and future plans.

Also, the organization needs strong leadership. There must be someone in charge who has the ability to inspire and motivate people into creative action. Strong leadership does not mean the ability to force others to submit to your will. Strong leadership means the ability to evoke new ideas and put them into action.

Because change almost always causes stress, the successful marketing manager must have a thorough knowledge of human relations. He must be capable of putting people in stress-causing situations and know how to maintain an effective organization. Very often this will mean accepting the role of psychologist and peace-maker.

Maintaining open lines of communication is a pre-requisite to having an effective marketing organization. The ability of a marketing organization to have undistorted multi-level communication with all interested parties is at best a difficult task. Marketing management, to be effective, must have facts. These facts must remain undistorted as they travel through the levels of management.

The marketing concept imposes one more very stringent requirement upon management. There must be complete acceptance of a system viewpoint. This means two things. First, it means that decisions must be made with the total organization in view. It means the integration of all departments into a single unified behaviour system. Visualizing this part of the systems concept is easy. Breaking down the individual jealousies and narrowmindedness of departmental thinking is very difficult.

The second point in accepting a systems approach is that the outside world must be brought into the internal system. There must be continuous feedback from the consumer behaviour system into the marketing organization's behaviour system. The marketing organization must learn to anticipate changes in consumer behaviour and have new operations ready when necessary. What this means is that management must have detailed information and knowledge about the behaviour system in which its product is sold.

We see that the marketing concept is not only a way of looking at customers. It imposes stringent rules of behaviour. Alderson and Green question how valid traditional management philosophies are when subjected to the marketing concept. Ranging from the most permissive to the most tightly controlled, the systems of management are: "Tuning up a Business to Run Itself, Management by Decision Rule, Management by Improvisation, Management by Exception, Management through Conflict and Management as a Negotiative Process."[4] According to Alderson and Green, the only management philosophy that is consistent with the needs of marketing is Management Through a Negotiative Process.

"Management as a Negotiative Process is the view that is favoured here ... It involves a disclosure of objectives which sound relationships with subordinates would appear to require. It lays the groundwork for direct, personal accountability for performance. It builds on the principle of two-way commitment in asserting that both sides should honour their commitments. Since a negotiated decision is a joint decision, it should be a dated decision—carrying the date that it was made and the date by when it is expected to be completed. It recognizes that objectives as well as methods can change. It is adapted to the spirit of the times both in its dynamic aspect and in the insistence that decision process should be made more formal and explicit."[5]

Marketing Management Functions

With a theoretical background of marketing and a review of marketing's place in the organization completed, let us look at the specific functions of marketing management. Many authors divide marketing functions into the following three areas: exchange, physical supply and facilitating functions. The exchange functions involve buying and selling. Transportation and storage are the physical supply functions. Finance, assumption of risk,

---

[4] Alderson and Green: *Planning & Problem Solving in Marketing*, Richard D. Irwin Inc., Homewood, Illinois, 1964, pp. 26-50.

[5] Ibid., p. 49.

pricing, standardization and gathering marketing data are the facilitating functions.

Describing the marketing functions in this way tends to perpetrate a narrow view of marketing. A wider managerial view of marketing would divide the marketing functions as follows: setting marketing objectives, developing the marketing plan, organizing the marketing function, putting the plan into action and controlling the marketing programme. Each managerial aspect of marketing must be considered when making decisions in the task-oriented marketing functions. Within each of these managerial functions, there are specific activities which I shall briefly outline.

Setting marketing objectives is basically a three-step process: determining consumer wants, segmenting the market and establishing specific objectives. The determination of consumer wants includes both an analysis of consumer motivation and establishment of the specific goods and services desired.

Market segmentation was first given meaning in the establishment of the trading area concept. Geographic areas were easily identifiable and provided a limited type of control. This type of limited segmentation has proved unsatisfactory for sophisticated marketing methodology. Later attempts at segmentation divided the market by population and income factors. Such things as age, sex, wealth and education level were considered vital. Slowly psychological and sociological factors have come into the segmentation approach. Some modern theorists in marketing are looking into factors such as family life cycle and family compatibility for clues to market segmentation.

Setting specific objectives will outline the quantitative aspect you wish to achieve. Objectives should be broad enough to allow room for individual creative effort but narrow enough to provide specific guidance. Success in achieving an objective is measured by payoff. Payoff should be expressed in a unit that indicates the extent to which an objective has been achieved.

Planning the marketing effort is often described as programming the specific activities involved in getting a product to market. One should expand the subject area to include those steps leading up to the programme and those tasks that remain after the programme has been launched. At this time no effort will be made to differentiate between planning for a new operation and market planning for an existing concern. There are differences in degree of emphasis between new and existing concerns but the overall structure remains the same.

You can spend considerable time evaluating the argument of

9

what comes first; the market plan or a statement of goals to be achieved by the market plan. Most people initially feel that a statement of goals and objectives must precede the market plan. There is a considerable body of opinion that says you are fooling yourself to think that you can measure the output of a market plan without first having some measure of the input. Resolution of the problem takes place when you state the process as follows—first there is a statement of desired objectives, then you measure the amount of input necessary to reach the objective. When optimum input is compared to actual input available, a market plan is developed which includes realistic and revised operating goals.

In actual planning, the first activity to take place should be a marketing audit. This audit will seek to find out what is unique about the company. More precisely, the audit is an inventory of corporate resources. Because a market plan will commit resources, it is essential for the planner to have complete knowledge of resource availability. In addition to assessing the availability of such physical assets as sales personnel, warehouse space, plant capacity and capital, the planner must consider less tangible things such as competition, customer relations and relationships with suppliers.

The second stage of planning is the development of strategies for consideration. At this point it would be appropriate to distinguish between four terms; strategy, tactics, plan and programme. Plans and strategies are used interchangeably; they refer to the broad outline of events to be achieved in reaching an objective. They are the individual items of success that when added together should result in an objective being reached. Tactics and programmes are the detailed steps to be taken in accomplishing the task of the strategy.

As tactics and programmes move down the heirarchy for implementation, they are used as strategies for developing even more detailed tactics. The tactics or programme that a sales manager presents to his sales force will become a guiding strategy for each man to follow with his own tactics.

The first phase of planning looks at the operation as it is. The second stage seeks ways to change and improve the operation. The generation of strategies is fundamental to planning. A market operation has as its purpose the implementation of a strategy.

Prime concern by market planners will not always be in the area of new plans and products. Identification of business opportunities should include re-appraisal of opportunities or strategies now being pursued.

10

Evaluating market opportunities will require the formulation of strategy statements in each of the following areas:
1. Depth of product line.
2. Product name and image.
3. Packaging.
4. Price.
5. Channels of distribution.
6. Physical distribution.
7. Selling effort.
8. Advertising content.

Making strategic decisions in the above areas will cause the following factors to be studied:
1. Product Specifications.
2. Market Estimates along with Price Volume Relationships.
3. Customers.
4. Sales Channels.
5. Competition.
6. Market Share Availability.
7. Manpower and Support Requirements.
8. Cost and Revenue tables.

The two lists just presented are not meant to be exhaustive. They are intended to give you a feeling for the complexity of any marketing decision. By its very nature, marketing cries out for control. Yet these very same factors of changeability and complexity make control most difficult. Control of the marketing effort is what makes marketing a system. Controls should be established to measure the effectiveness of the marketing effort. These same controls should also provide a basis for planning new marketing efforts.

The critical role marketing plays within an individual company carries itself forward to the entire economy. Personal consumption expenditures, which are the direct result of marketing effort, account for over fifty percent of the total value of goods and services produced in the economy. Gross National Product, which is a reflection of the total value of all goods and services produced, gives some idea of the importance of marketing to the economy. But, when one looks at the G.N.P. very closely, he sees that the type of accounting used grossly understates the total dollar value of all transactions taking place in the economy. As one gains an understanding of national income accounting, he begins to realize that the country's marketing system must handle a volume of goods and services well in excess of that shown as the final Gross National Product. Marketing could honestly be called the delivery system for your standard of living.

11

DISCUSSION QUESTIONS

1. Discuss the development of the marketing concept.
2. What place does market information play in marketing management?
3. What macro and micro-environmental factors create the need for new products?
4. What requirements does the marketing concept impose on marketing management?
5. Describe the job of marketing management.

BIBLIOGRAPHY

ALDERSON & GREEN: *Planning and Problem Solving in Marketing,* Richard D. Irwin Inc., Homewood, Ill., U.S.A., 1964.

ALEXANDER & BERG: *Dynamic Management in Marketing,* Richard D. Irwin Inc., Homewood, Ill., U.S.A., 1965.

BECKMAN & DAVIDSON: *Marketing,* Ronald Press, New York, N.Y., U.S.A., 7th Ed., 1965.

BRITT & BOYD: *Marketing Management and Administrative Action,* McGraw-Hill, New York, N.Y., U.S.A., 1963.

HOWARD: *Marketing Management: Analysis and Planning,* Richard D. Irwin, Homewood, Ill., U.S.A.

KELLY: *Marketing Strategy and Functions,* Prentice-Hall, Englewood Cliffs, N.J., U.S.A., 1965.

LEVITT: *Innovation in Marketing,* McGraw-Hill, New York, N.Y., U.S.A., 1962.

MCCARTHY: *Basic Marketing—A Managerial Approach,* Richard D. Irwin Inc., Homewood, Ill., U.S.A., 1964.

STAUT & TAYLOR: *A Managerial Introduction to Marketing,* Prentice-Hall, Englewood Cliffs, N.J., U.S.A.

2

The Market Transaction

A MARKET transaction takes place when there has been a successful matching of buyer and seller. The power of either party to influence a transaction's outcome is often described in terms of competitive strength. This competitive strength is derived in some way from the competitive structure of the industry in which the transaction takes place. Economists have developed classical models for various competitive structures. In an effort to more fully understand the power of the marketing organization, a review of each of the models is necessary.

The actual market transaction takes place after a specified series of events has been completed. In order to minimize the costs of completing this series of events, the marketing manager must understand the interrelationships between each event. This will require looking at much more than the immediate buyer-seller relationship. A conceptual framework can be developed for looking at the market transaction. It is within this framework that the marketing manager should analyze and plan his company's efforts.

Economic Models and Their Influence on Marketing Decisions

Classical economic models move in a series of steps from perfect competition to pure monopoly. This discussion will cover the broadest outlines of each model and will be concerned with how the model can be used to shape marketing decisions. The classical model applied to any industry will depend on the structure of the industry and the nature of the actual competition that takes place.

13

Agricultural markets are often referred to as examples of perfect competition. It should therefore be obvious from the beginning of this discussion that the economist's name for a model should not carry a value judgement. The prerequisites for perfect competition are five related factors. There should be a homogeneous supply so that one seller's supply cannot be preferred to his competitor's. Trading for the product takes place in an organized market, so that trading is continuous and there is perfect dissemination of information providing sellers and buyers with the result of every transaction. Each seller should be too small to have any effect on the supply of the product offered for sale; therefore the seller cannot have an effect on the price of the product. Also the number of buyers should be so large that no single buyer can affect the supply or price. The fourth prerequisite is that there shall be no restraints on the independence of buyers and sellers. Last and most important is the nature of price in perfect competition. At any single instant of time there must be a uniform price, but over a period of time the price must be flexible enough to reflect changes in supply and demand.

For the firm operating under conditions of perfect competition, marketing management would come close to being a contradiction in terms. Management implies the freedom to make a decision. The only decision available to the above marketing manager is whether or not to sell his product. Any attempt to differentiate his product from competitors' would be wasted effort and would only add to his costs.

Pure competition comes close to perfect competition in its scope for management action. Pure competition is identical to "perfect" in its treatment of standard commodities, number and size of buyers and sellers and individual control over price. Where the two concepts diverge is in their treatment of information, capital flows and independence of action. Pure competition allows for an unequal distribution of supply and demand information as long as the inequality is not artificially contrived. Custom may not allow complete freedom of action and capital flows are sometimes less free than in perfect competition. As we can see, the marketing manager is still a victim of his environment with very little control over his product.

Imperfect competition is the name economists give to any competitive situation that is not "perfect" or "pure". It may be monopolistic competition, oligopoly, collusion, one of the types of self-destructive competition or monopoly. In general, imperfect competition involves serious deviations from the "ideal" models. Information flows may be imperfect with specific information kept secret from segments of the trading population. Independence of action may be limited by fear or restrictive agreements. Severe limitations may be placed on the mobility of capital with entrance and exit from an industry being hindered. Real or imagined product differences will prevent free switching between buyers and sellers. Finally, buyers and sellers may be large enough to have serious effects on supply and demand; thereby having a direct influence on price.

Monopolistic competition is the form of imperfect competition resulting from product differentiation. Sellers differentiate their product so that buyers hesitate before switching allegiance because of price differentials. Price differences will exist to the point where another product can be substituted at equal or lower cost. Monopolistic competition allows sellers to compete in quality, service, fashion, promotion and price. The type of market place created by monopolistic competition is most closely related to reality. It is the type of market place in which the marketing manager can make decisions about each part of the marketing mix. In other words, he has freedom in choosing his channel of distribution, price, advertising, selling approach and any other marketing tool.

Oligopoly and collusion can be stated as the effect of few sellers. Oligopoly exists when the number of sellers is so few that increases or decreases in production will seriously affect the market price.

Commodities may be standardized or differentiated. Each producer will give serious consideration to possible repercussions if he changes price. The results of oligopoly look as if collusion were present. This is often not the case although industry prices tend to change with complete harmony. Non-price factors are most often used to gain competitive advantage, although price should be, and is part of, the effective range of marketing decisions.

Harmony in price changes under oligopoly can be caused by price leadership. This type of price co-ordination takes place in the absence of any collusion. The leader firm in the industry adjusts price and there is an almost simultaneous price change throughout the industry. Leadership can be of either the dominant or barometric type. Dominant leadership exists when there is one large firm and a peripheral edge of competitors. The smaller firms can usually sell their entire production at the leader's price so there is no reason to undercut. Stability in the industry depends on the leader's ability to judge overall demand. Barometric leadership occurs because the remainder of the industry feels the leader has properly judged a change in demand conditions.

According to Howard, in *Marketing Management: Analysis and Planning,* collusion can take three forms: perfect, limited and effective. Perfect collusion is the most restrictive type of collusion. It requires complete co-ordination on all competitive fronts. Price is identical, sales quotas are mutually decided upon and production may be shared. Effective collusion exists when companies set identical prices, share the market, but compete on a non-price basis with product research, advertising and salesmen. Effective collusion would be typical of the European cartel system. Limited collusion applies to those cases where there is intermittent rivalry and agreement. It occurs when fuller collusion is not possible because of the corporate personalities involved.

The extent of the collusion taking place will govern the marketing manager's freedom. Effective and limited collusion do not cover non-price decisions, and some degree of dynamic managment is possible. Truly effective management will have a tendency to destroy collusive agreements.

Destructive competition occurs when prices are cut so far that no one can recover costs or make a fair return on investment. Price wars usually create situations of destructive competition. Successive price cuts occur when companies fail to understand their interrelationship. They may also be caused when companies feel they are strong enough to withstand all competitive price changes.

Monopoly is the economist's opposite for perfect competition. A company is a monopolist when it is the sole seller of a particular commodity. Because there are few, if any, identical products in our industrial complex, almost every producer is a type of monopolist. In the theoretical case, a monopolist has complete freedom to set his price at the point where he will maximize profits. Monopoly powers in the real world end at the extremes of price that will cause product substitution.

Reviewing the economist's competitive models, we see eight basic factors or structural differences that govern the degree and type of competition. These eight factors are:
1. The number and size of firms selling in the market.
2. Degree of product differentiation.
3. Industry demand.
4. Size and number of buyers.
5. Market channels employed.

6. Nature of costs.
7. Geographic dimensions.
8. Law

Summarizing the effects on price of these eight factors, we come up with the following generalizations:

1. The fewer the number of firms, the less likely price will be used as a competitive tool.
2. True differences in product will allow price differences to develop without chaotic competition resulting.
3. Collusion is most prevalent in the downward portion of the business cycle.
4. Large knowledgeable buyers will force price competition.
5. The longer the market channel, the more chance for price competition to exist.
6. High fixed costs and stable raw materials costs are likely to discourage price competition.
7. Geographic isolation can cause competitive isolation.
8. Laws to encourage competition will hinder written collusive agreements but will not stop effective or limited collusion.[1]

The Heterogeneous Market

The economist proposes a completely homogeneous product when describing perfect competition. Wroe Alderson has developed a theory of perfectly heterogeneous markets which he claims is more closely related to reality.

"Organized behaviour systems are the entities which operate in the marketing environment. The nature of that environment is suggested by the concept of the heterogeneous market. A perfectly heterogeneous market would be one in which there was a precise match between differentiated units of supply and differentiated segments of demand. At the same time it is recognized that partial homogeneities exist throughout the marketing system and that one of the functions of the system is to produce these partial homogeneities."[2]

Heterogeneous markets need not be perfect. There may be and usually is a large degree of imbalance. Buyers may demand products not available and sellers may provide unwanted products. These imbalances may be removed by product or marketing innovation. It is this imbalance which makes marketing a dynamic force.

---

1 Howard: *Marketing Management: Analysis & Planning*, Richard D. Irwin Inc., Homewood Ill., Rev. Ed., 1963, pp. 144-170.

2 Wroe Alderson: *Dynamic Marketing Behaviour*—Richard D. Irwin Inc., Homewood, Ill., 1965, p. 26.

In the perfectly heterogeneous market the matching of individual segments of supply and demand can only take place through the availability of perfect information. Alderson presents the heterogeneous market as a tool for describing the information problem. The economist reduces all information to a statement of price. Alderson proposes that price is only one part of the information picture presented to the consumer.

Differential Advantage

Pairing of buyers and sellers in a purely homogeneous market would take place on a random basis. The effort to reduce this type of matching process and increase the selective type of matching has led to the need for differential advantage. Today we can say that almost every firm occupies a somewhat unique position. By making most of its individual nature the firm seeks to establish a competitive advantage.

Chamberlain has stated the economics of differential advantages as follows:

"A general class of products is differentiated if any significant basis exists for distinguishing the goods (or service) of one seller from those of another ... where such differentiation exists, even though it be slight, buyers will be paired with sellers, not by chance and at random as under pure competition, but according to their preferences."[3]

The individual firm can seek and maintain differential advantage in five ways.

1. Market Segmentation
2. Selective Appeals
3. Product Improvement
4. Process Improvement
5. Product Innovation[4]

To gain differential advantage through market segmentation, the business firm selects a group of customers with relatively homogeneous demands out of an area of consumer use which is heterogeneous in the aggregate. Limiting production to the range demanded by a selected group of consumers will allow production efficiencies. The scale of operation necessary to obtain production efficiency can often lead to an increase in selling expenses. This last point is mentioned so as to stop any thoughts that would lead to the conclusion that differential advantage is obtained at no cost. One cost peculiar to the drive for product differentiation is partial customer alienation. By

---

[3] Chamberlain: *Theory of Monopolistic Competition*, Harvard Univ. Press, Cambridge, Massachusetts, 6th Ed., 1950.
[4] Alderson: op cit, pp. 184-210.

appealing to any single group need, it is almost automatic that you will neglect or refute the needs of customers to whom you are not directly appealing.

Differentiation can occur through advertising without any change in product. By choosing customers whose demands he can satisfy and using selective appeals in advertising, the seller can set up a circle of reinforcement. The cost of analyzing and choosing selective appeals will again tend to offset production efficiencies.

The remaining three avenues to differential advantage are all variations on product differentiation. Product improvement, product innovation and process improvement may create advantage in product, patent, trade mark, trade name, package, quality, colour, design, conditions surrounding sales, distribution, warehousing and inventory control. Enterprise differentiation is the name given to the last four listed factors.

Product improvement is the method producers use to maintain their relative industrial position and to provide customers with the newest in technology. The improvement may or may not be incorporated in advertising. It would seem foolish to advertise that you have removed one of your product's weak points.

Innovation in a product is the step taken to gain advantage in a new market or to stem the tide of competition. Differential advantage is neutralized over time through competitive action. Interfirm differences create new opportunities for competition through simulation, deviation and complementation.

Process improvement is a more permanent and rewarding development in the drive for differential advantage. Through patent protection on a process, competition is forced to use less economical production methods, pay a royalty or refrain from producing. Any of these three outcomes leaves the leading firm in a strong competitive position.

Dynamics of Market Opportunity

The quest for differential advantage is engaged upon to provide the firm with a degree of monopoly power. For an economy to be dynamic, it must meet the needs of consumers. The monopoly power of differential advantage would be unwanted if it proved a barrier to dynamic growth. Fortunately, the successful achievement of differential advantage provides the stimulus for more growth. The proliferation of opportunity is the natural outgrowth of a free expanding economy.

The successful innovator in an industry provides stimulation for new firms to compete by simulation. Without incurring the cost of pioneering, the second, third and following entrants into an industry can copy the leader and choose small segments of demand they are able to sell profitably. The lower the capital requirements for entry, the more danger of direct simulation to the innovator.

As was mentioned earlier, the search for differential advantage will alienate some portion of the possible consuming market. By adopting some particular set of appeals the innovator opens the path to competition through deviation. The follower in this case chooses to appeal to the group of customers whom the innovator has decided to ignore.

In the third opportunity-creating situation provided by differential advantage, the new firm takes over part of the innovator's function. The proliferation of new industry creates its own demand for service institutions. Complementation will provide the stimulus for new industry as long as the complementary firm can do a better and more economical job than the industry it services.

The Process of Exchange[5]

So far we have been dealing with macro-factors in the exchange process. The entire macro-process is carried out through the micro-organism of the individual transaction. It is necessary to understand both aspects of exchange and their relationship to marketing decisions.

In the earlier discussion it was pointed out that marketing attempted to match segments of supply and demand. What is the factor that brings these two market segments together? Stated simply, the matching process takes place to increase the utility of the assortment held by each party to a transaction.

In very few cases is the matching of supply and demand accomplished between raw material producer and final consumer. The matching process takes place through a series of sorting operations which slowly bring the product to its final user. Sorting-out, accumulating, allocating and assorting are the four steps found to be present in the marketing of most goods.

If you assume that the economic process starts with a heterogeneous supply of raw materials, sorting out is the step that breaks this conglomeration down into homogeneous groups that

---

5 See note at the end of this chapter.

are meaningful to the sorter. For example, the egg farmer would be sorting out when he divided the productive effort of his hens into various grades and sizes. The division into meaningful groups will depend on the availability of standards.

Once there has been the initial sorting-out, the small homogeneous groups from many different areas can be brought together in the form of accumulations. The service provided by grain elevators or similar marketing intermediaries performs the accumulation function. Physical placement of the accumulation is a critical problem and will depend on investment requirements, perishability of the product and physical storage requirements. A final point to be made is that a single marketing intermediary may provide an accumulating service for many products.

Allocation of accumulated goods is both an internal and external problem. Internally the firm allocates its accumulated storage of raw materials, labour and capital in an effort to maximize productive efficiency. External allocation of production or sales should be accomplished with due attention being paid to the economists' theory of marginal revenue. Very often the theoretical optimum of matching marginal revenue and marginal cost in the allocation problem is never reached. Reasons for this failure will become clear at a later time.

Household and industrial purchasing agents build assortments in an effort to be prepared for all demands. The household purchasing agent chooses goods from the accumulation provided in retail stores. She or he does this in anticipation of family consumption needs. Industrial purchasing agents, while buying on a much larger scale, perform the same function. The variety of goods held in the consumer's possession is an assortment. This same assortment can be visualized as an accumulation if there is to be further allocation.

It is the "transaction" that moves a product through the sorting procedure just described. The transaction is the result of the double search in which consumers look for goods and services, and suppliers look for customers. The two groups exchange information and through implicit or explicit negotiation agree on terms of sale.

It is important to draw a distinction between fully negotiated and routine transactions. Fully negotiated transactions are those required to deal with a unique or non-recurring situation. They are often of strategic importance. Full negotiation can spell out the framework for many routine negotiations that follow. The fully negotiated transaction may also be of strategic importance because of the large amount of capital involved in relation to total corporate resources.

Reducing transactions to routine is a basic way of achieving marketing economy. Transactions must be highly repetitive in nature and stable in character if real economies are to be achieved. Stated in basic terms, routine transactions take place according to pre-accepted rules and require minimal discussion on terms of trade.

It was stated earlier that the matching of supply and demand had as its purpose an increase in the utility of the assortment held by both parties to the transaction. Wroe Alderson has expressed this idea in formula form.

> "In the expression $X \simeq Y$, it is merely asserted that X is exchanged for Y ... Given that X is an element of the assortment A_1 and Y is an element of the assortment A_2, X is exchangeable for Y if, and only if, these three conditions hold!
> a. X is different from Y.
> b. The potency of the assortment A_1 is increased by dropping X and adding Y.
> c. The potency of the assortment A_2 is increased by adding X and dropping Y.
> In symbols, the law of exchange would be stated as follows:
> $X \simeq Y$, if and only if $X \neq Y(X \epsilon A_1$ and $Y \epsilon A_2)$
> $P(A_1 - X + Y) > PA_1$ and $P(A_2 + X - Y) > PA_2$
> The previous formulation makes no explicit reference to the cost of executing an exchange transaction. For a complete statement of the Law of Exchange, it shall be stated explicitly that the increased potency for the assortment A_1 is brought about by the transaction, and that the same thing should be true of assortment A_2. This corollary of the Law of Exchange might be stated symbolically as follows:
> $X \simeq$ implies that $C[P(A_1 - X + Y) - P(A_1)] > CA_1(Tr)$
> $\qquad\qquad\qquad C[P(A_2 + X - Y) - P(A_2)] > CA_2(Tr)$"[6]

Alderson also proposes that you can add an infinite number of intermediaries between producer and consumer as long as the optimality of each transaction is maintained. "Transvection" is the name given to the unit of action or the system which a product moves through during its sorts and transformations on its way to consumers. Transvections are optimal if costs cannot be decreased by either increasing or decreasing the number of steps. To repeat an earlier statement, the marketing manager must look far beyond the immediate buyer-seller relationship for a framework within which to make decisions.

---

6 Ibid, p. 84.

Note

The reader will note that the portion of this chapter entitled "The Process of Exchange" is in large part a discussion of information contained in two books by Wroe Alderson: *Dynamic Marketing Behaviour* and *Marketing Behaviour and Executive Action*. Professor Alderson is one of the few men to treat the transaction problem. Both books are published by Richard D. Irwin Inc., Homewood, Illinois, U.S.A.

DISCUSSION QUESTIONS

1. Compare and contrast perfect, pure and monopolistic competition.
2. What competitive situations precipitate simultaneous price changes? Describe the evolution of these competitive structures.
3. What is differential advantage and how does it create opportunities for expanding market opportunity?
4. Discuss marketing as a process of sorts and matches.
5. Describe the requirements necessary for a transaction to take place.

BIBLIOGRAPHY

ALDERSON: *Marketing Behavior and Executive Action*, Richard D. Irwin Inc., Homewood, Ill., U.S.A.

ALDERSON: *Dynamic Marketing Behavior*, Richard D. Irwin Inc., Homewood, Ill., U.S.A., 1965.

CHAMBERLAIN: *Theory of Monopolistic Competition*, Harvard University Press, Cambridge, Mass., U.S.A., 6th Ed.

DEAN: *Managerial Economics*, Prentice-Hall, Englewood Cliffs, N.J., U.S.A.

HOWARD: *Marketing Management: Analysis and Planning*, Richard D. Irwin Inc., Homewood, Ill., U.S.A.

3

Consumer Behaviour

THE term marketing implies a relationship between producer and consumer. The nature of this relationship is determined by the behaviour patterns of both parties. Appreciation and understanding of the factors involved in determining consumer behaviour are necessary for effective marketing management. This chapter will attempt to cover the more important determinants of consumer behaviour. We will develop a model of consumer behaviour in the purchase situation. We will also cover the most promising techniques available for measuring and forecasting consumer behaviour.

Consumer Behaviour: Rational versus Irrational

Does the consumer enter the market place as a rational decision-maker or is he the slave of irrational impulses and drives? There is almost no evidence to support a hypothesis of irrational consumer behaviour. Rather, there is a large body of theory and experimental data that shows the consumer enters the market as a rational decision-maker.

Consumer purchasing patterns are no less rational than any other human behaviour pattern. They are shaped by a multitude of physical and mental needs. These needs are determined by the individual and his relationship to the community. "Relatively little of what most people strive for most of the time is necessary for sheer survival . . . especially in societies where basic physical needs are amply provided for; and what much of what many people want and do seems unrelated or even detrimental to their physical welfare. . . . Even the behaviour that does stem directly from the needs of the body and for the

24

species, such as eating, having sexual relations or caring for the young, is not controlled nearly so directly by physiological needs as in the case of lower animals."[1] If physiological needs leave a great deal of human behaviour unexplained, other types of motives must produce the majority of human behaviour. These other motives are: "secondary, learned, social or psychogenic".[2]

The word motive has been used several times and should be defined to avoid confusion. "A motive is the inner state that energizes, activates, or moves, . . . and that directs or channels behaviour toward goals."[3] Goal-directed behaviour and a realization that motivation need not be physiological has led to the development of reference group theory. "The concept has been particularly useful in accounting for the choices made among apparent alternatives, particularly where the selections seem to be contrary to the best interests of the actor. . . . One common usage of the concept is in designation of that group which serves as the point of reference in making comparisons or contrasts, especially in forming judgements about one's self. . . . A second referent of the concept is that group in which the actor aspires to gain or maintain acceptance. . . . In a third usage the concept signifies that group whose perspectives constitute the frame of reference for the actor."[4] It would seem that the last definition of reference group would be most meaningful to marketing management.

Culture and Human Behaviour

Man's largest reference group which seems to have any significance for the study of human behaviour and its influence on marketing is his culture. The classical definition of culture is . . . "that complex whole which includes knowledge, belief, art, law, morals and any other habits acquired by man as a member of society. . . . Whatever else may be said about it, culture is always first of all the product of men in groups: a set of ideas, attitudes, and habits—rules if one will—evolved by men to help them in their conduct of life."[5]

"In short it is fair to say that whereas all human behaviour

---

[1] Berelson and Steiner, *Human Behaviour, An Inventory of Scientific Findings,* Harcourt, Brace & World, New York, 1964, p. 48.
[2] Ibid., p. 240.
[3] Ibid., p. 240.
[4] Tomotsu Shibutani, *Reference Groups as Perspectives in Marketing and the Behavioural Sciences,* Allyn & Bacon, Boston, 1963, pp. 220-222.
[5] Zaltman, *Marketing, Contributions from the Behavioural Sciences,* Harcourt, Brace & World, New York, 1965, p. 7.

is in some sense physiologically or biologically based, only a small part of it is physiologically or biologically determined. For the rest, there are the perceptions, the definitions of the situation, the interpretations, the values, the responses, the manners, the language, the religions and the philosophies that are given at any moment by the culture."[6]

According to Edward Hall in his book, *The Silent Language*,[7] there are ten ways in which culture expresses itself. These ten cultural message systems provide clues for marketing management in its communication with customers.

Interaction: Physical communication in the form of speech and print is culture's most common form of interaction. The meaning attached to words can change between cultures. The accepted pace of interaction can vary along with its degree of formality. Before selling in a new culture, it is necessary to have a full understanding of its patterns of interaction.

Associations: Human beings belong to a variety of formal and informal groups. Behaviour patterns within groups have significant meaning to marketing. The behaviour of small groups will be covered at a later point. It should suffice to say that cultural differences in forms of association create numerous marketing problems.

Subsistence: The level of economic development in a culture will govern its acceptance and rejection of new products. Economic development will govern what types of messages are accepted or rejected by the culture. Products considered necessities in one culture will be rejected as luxuries that cannot be afforded at a lower level of development.

Bisexuality: The relationships between men and women differ from culture to culture. Female or male activities accepted by one culture may be completely rejected by another. Marketing appeals must not reverse the male-female role within a culture.

Territoriality: Cultures establish physical boundaries to regulate certain types of activities. These boundaries, at their lowest level, exist within the family. They also exist for the entire culture. Neighbourhood development would be an example of how the culture establishes physical boundaries.

Temporality: Time patterns vary between cultures. The value of time spent in business and leisure can cause severe frustrations for firms entering a new culture. Time dimensions vary within the family. The family life cycle can change between cultures.

---

6 Berelson, op. cit., pp. 645-646.
7 Hall, *The Silent Language,* Fawcett World Library, New York, 1961.

26

Learning: The institutions and patterns of learning are not universal. Cultural differences in the dissemination of information will pose many problems for marketing management.

Play: Cultures vary in how they engage in play. The time, place and type of game played will vary in addition to culture's attitudes towards play.

Defence: Individuals and cultures have defence requirements. Clothing, medicine and shelter are only some of the individual's defence assortment. Cultures defend themselves with police forces, armies and laws. Again, attitudes toward defence will vary between cultures.

Exploitation: Each culture exploits its assets in a variety of ways. The willingness of a society to adopt particular forms of exploitation will determine the feasibility of various marketing plans.

If the marketing manager will look to these ten message systems before attempting to do business in a new culture, serious errors can be avoided. Cultures are made up of many smaller subcultures or groups. Certain attributes of group behaviour seem to have universality. We will look at some of these attributes for clues to the solution of marketing problems.

Group Behaviour and Marketing

Berelson and Steiner, in their chapter on opinions, attitudes and beliefs (O.A.B.'s), review how various group memberships alter individual O.A.B.'s. Berelson and Steiner are interested in how O.A.B.'s develop and how they change. We will therefore review some of their findings.

O.A.B.'s that originate in earlier periods persist into later time periods. Put into terms of importance to marketing: O.A.B.'s about a product will live longer than the actual truth of the matter. Bad impressions will last long after a bad product has been changed and improved. Favourable public opinion will not change in immediate response to product deterioration.

"People hold O.A.B.'s in harmony with their group memberships and identifications. A basic finding in social psychology is that the attitudes a person holds depend in part upon his social contacts and particularly upon the groups in which he holds membership . . . It becomes apparent that the consumer faced with a baffling array of brands . . . with untold possibilities on his television dial makes choices which are not based primarily on the inherent merits of the object chosen, no matter how persuasively these merits may have been advertised to them. It further appears that these choices are widely affected, not alone by the choice object itself or by the advertising and propaganda about it, but also by other people . . . Thus his reactions are not random relative to the reactions of these others. His perception and responses form part of a pattern of interaction and mutual orientations among all members of the group."[8]

O.A.B.'s within a group are primarily influenced by the most respected members of the group, the opinion leaders. Opinion leaders will tend to be a little better educated than the group but not so much so that they are out of contact with the group. The leader is the model for opinion within the group. Opinion leaders within a group will differ by subject of leadership. "The more communications are directed to the group's opinion leaders rather than to the rank-and-file members, the more effective they are likely to be."[9]

In addition to the opinion leader, there is one other person in an opinion-controlling position, the gatekeeper. A gatekeeper is a person who controls a strategic portion of a channel for the flow of products, services or ideas into a group "so as to have the power of decision over whether whatever is flowing through the channel will enter the group or not."[10] The interaction between opinion leader and gatekeeper is critical to the acceptance of an idea by a group.

Social Class

"Every known human society, certainly every known society of any size, is stratified. The hierarchical evaluation of people in different social positions is apparently inherent in human social organization. Stratification arises with the most rudimentary division of labour and appears to be socially necessary in order to get people to fill different positions and perform adequately in them."[11]

If we accept a person's social class as one of the groups he belongs to, then social class becomes an important marketing consideration. Social class norms and modes of behaviour will directly affect the success of a marketing programme. Saxon Graham has studied social class in its relation to the acceptance of innovation.[12] We will review some of his findings.

Graham's hypothesis was as follows: "Social classes will

8 Berelson, op. cit., pp. 566-567.
9 Ibid., p. 50.
10 Katz and Lazerfield, *Personal Influence,* New York Free Press, Glenco, New York, 1955, p. 119.
11 Berelson, op. cit., p. 460.
12 Saxon Graham, "Class and Conservatism in the Adoption of Innovations", *Human Relations,* Vol. IX, No. 1, 1956, pp. 91-100.

accept innovations to the extent that the innovational features and the cultural characteristics of the classes are compatible. Because they vary in many aspects of their culture, different classes will possibly adopt a given innovation in varying degrees. But because they share some aspects of common culture, they may accept in no significant degree. Finally, because each innovation requires that those who would use it should possess different physical, mental and behavioural equipment, no class could be said to be conservative or liberal in reacting to all."[13] Graham then goes on to show that each point in his hypothesis is true. His final statement is that the relationship between class and conservatism is more complex than realized. We can only re-emphasize this point. Social class reaction to a particular product can only serve as a partial guide to their acceptance of other products.

Pierre Martineau has studied the relationship between social class and spending behaviour. He reports the following conclusions:

"1. There is a social class system operative in metropolitan markets which can be isolated and described.
2. It is important to realize that there are far-reaching psychological differences between the various classes . . .
3. Consumption patterns operate as prestige symbols to define class membership, which is a more significant determinant of economic behaviour than mere income."[14]

For the marketing manager to neglect social class implications in a decision would be a grievous mistake. Social class alone will not explain consumer behaviour but it puts light into a grey area.

Family

Many reasons exist for the family being of prime interest to the marketing manager. Its primary importance is that it is one of an individual's most important reference groups. Secondly, the pattern of life within a family, and its place in the family life cycle, regulates many purchase decisions. We have already had a quick look at reference groups. This next section will examine the family life cycle and behaviour patterns within the family.

The concept of a family life cycle is not particularly difficult

---

13 Ibid., p. 92.
14 Pierre Martineau, "Social Class and Spending Behaviour", *Journal of Marketing,* National quarterly publication of the American Marketing Association, Vol. 23, Oct. 1958, p. 130

to understand. The life cycle begins at birth and has breaking points at marriage, continues through the life of the partners in the marriage and ends with the death of each partner. The family life cycle is subdivided by the birth of children, the departure of the children from the family and the death of a spouse. Within each of these broad classifications sub-clauses exist, such as: young marrieds with oldest children over ten.

An interesting study, done by Lansing and Kish at the University of Michigan, contrasted the results of studying purchase patterns by family life cycle and age of head of family. The study looked at such factors as home ownership, debts, wife working, income, purchase of new car and purchase of television. The family life cycle was divided as follows: young single, young married no children, young married youngest child under six, young married youngest child six or older, older married children, older single, others. For a breakdown of age of head of family the study started with eighteen-year-olds with groupings as follows: 18-24, 25-34, 35-44, 45-54, 55-64, 65+.[15]

The study was significant because it showed wide variations in results between the age study and the family life cycle study. In each case the family life cycle results were more sensitive and more meaningful to a marketing manager. The age group results tended to mask and smooth out many variations in purchase patterns.

Wroe Alderson presents an interesting problem when he talks about the four classifications of co-ordination and compatibility in the family: co-ordinated and compatible, co-ordinated and incompatible, unco-ordinated and compatible, unco-ordinated and incompatible.[16] For a complete understanding of this concept, it is necessary to distinguish between two types of behaviour: congenial and instrumental. Congenial behaviour is activity engaged in for its own satisfaction. Playing games with no monetary reward would be an example. Instrumental behaviour on the other hand has some specific goal attached to it. In his co-operation compatibility comparisons, Alderson is looking at compatibility of congenial behaviour and the co-operation in instrumental behaviour between husband and wife.

The unco-ordinated incompatible family is one where wife and husband find no enjoyment in each other and their values

---

15 Lansing and Kish, "Family Life Cycle as an Independent Variable", *American Sociological Review*, Oct. 1957, pp. 512-519.
16 Alderson, *Marketing Behaviour*, op. cit., p. 177.

towards money do not match reality. The unco-ordinated but compatible family will live together in harmony but there will never be any money in the bank to meet unexpected expenses. Co-ordinated incompatible families realize their economic obligations but find no enjoyment in each other. Finally, the co-ordinated compatible family enjoy life together and have an equal understanding of financial responsibility.

In addition to presenting a new way of looking at family behaviour, Alderson sounds a warning: family conflict patterns are often not taken into consideration in motivation research. The role of each person in the family changes, depending on the type of conflict in the family. Motivation research must adjust its research techniques to allow a proper understanding of family units on a co-operation-compatibility basis.

Consumer Behaviour and the Acceptance of Innovation

We have already mentioned the importance of innovation to corporate life. A good deal of research has been directed towards tracing the process of innovation acceptance. Understanding consumer behaviour has no more important application than in the innovation process. The process of accepting innovation is similar to learning. We must therefore review the learning process. Finally, some of the effects of mass communication on the acceptance of innovation will be looked at.

Learning is defined as follows: "Changes in behaviour that result from previous behaviour in similar situations (as opposed to changes due to physiological variations such as growth, deterioration, hunger, fatigue, alcohol or sleep). Mostly, by no means always, behaviour becomes demonstrably more effective and more adaptive after the exercise than it was before. In the broadest terms, then, learning refers to the effects of experience, either direct or symbolic, on subsequent behaviour."[17]

From the above definition, it is obvious that the seller of a new product must make the customers learn before the customer will buy the new product. In behavioural terms, the seller is attempting to change a response through the introduction of new stimuli. The ultimate desire is to create a habit which is a connection between stimuli and response that is virtually automatic.

The stimuli portion of learning is made up of a motive and a cue. Motives are the basic drives that we are attempting to

17 Berelson, op. cit., p. 135.

satisfy. The cue is the specific stimuli which triggers a specific response. After response there is either positive or negative reinforcement. Negative reinforcement will cause us to change our response to the specific cue. Positive reinforcement, which is the result of satisfactorily reaching our goal, will act as a conditioning agent in producing habit.

"There is an interrelationship among the fundamental learning factors. Cues are the distinctive characteristics of a product or innovation. If the value of these cues is highly esteemed then the amount of reward perceived is correspondingly high. The customer perceives the cues of an innovation as a means of reducing the drive."[18] Cues can take the form of any of a product's characteristics: brand name, package, price, colour, etc. Any of these cues can serve to trigger a response.

The ability of a cue to elicit any response will depend on a customer's perception of that particular cue. Perception is the process by which we select, organize and interpret sensory stimulation into meaningful and coherent pictures. There are thousands of stimuli acting upon us at all times. The choice of these we perceive is not a random sample of the available stimuli. The stimuli selected depend on the stimuli, our previous experience or learning in relation to the stimuli and our motives which are strongest at that particular time.

Let us assume that a potential customer perceives your new product. If a series of other factors are correct, the potential customer may become an actual customer. It is quite obvious that some customers will purchase new products sooner than others. It has been possible to identify certain characteristics with early and late adoption of innovations. The research in this field to date has dealt primarily with small groups of non-consumer items. The one study done on a very large selection of products was concerned in the main with mobility characteristics. It seems reasonable to assume the factors so far identified are correct but more research into the adoption process is necessary before it can be left in peace.

"The first group of people to adopt an innovation are called 'innovators'. This is the group that is most apt to make risky decisions. They are typically the youngest group in age and the highest in social status and wealth. Innovators rely heavily on impersonal and scientific information sources and communication with other innovators. In their social relationships innovators are often opinion leaders as well. They are frequently

---

18 Zaltman, op. cit., p. 21.

cosmopolites; they have professional, business or social contacts outside their immediate social circle."[19]

The next group consists of early adopters. These people are also of high social status. They are most likely to hold elected office and be opinion leaders. This group is less cosmopolite than the innovators and they get a large amount of information from salesmen. Innovators and early adopters tend to be more creative than later adopters.

In a study of mobility characteristics, the Opinion Research Corporation found the following characteristics in early innovators: "They travel more and change residence more often. They show more movement through occupational and economic levels. They associate with a wider variety of people of different types. They move through more educational levels and institutions. They read more and in general move through more intellectual influences."[20]

Although early acceptors are generally more mobile and more creative than later acceptors, refinement of the concept is necessary for marketing management. It has been found that consumers who are interest-committed to the general area of innovation will be amongst the earliest adopters. Joining the two points, we find a more workable marketing tool that says early adopters will be more mobile, of higher status, etc., and will already have an interest in the general product class.

The last three groups of product acceptors are the early majority, late majority and the laggards. Early and late majority contain about seventy per cent of the total market, split evenly between the two. The early majority will not accept a product until opinion leaders have expressed themselves. They are still above average in social status and have considerable contact with salesmen.

Average social status and income seems to be representative of the late majority. They depend very heavily on the early majority for opinion leadership. Mass media is not an important source of information.

Laggards are societies' tradition-bound lower status groups. By the time laggards accept a product it has usually been superseded by another innovation. One exception in the low status groups is the relatively well-to-do member who accepts every innovation in an attempt to raise his status.

New thoughts about the role of communications in product

19 Ibid., p. 18.
20 "America's Tastemakers", *Research Report 1*, Vol. 17, Princeton: N.J. Opinion Research Corp., N.Y., 1959, p. 46.

innovation have resulted from the study of adopter groups. For certain groups there is complete dependence on printed matter, while others depend on personal opinion, mass media or a combination of communication services. Opinion leaders depend most heavily on impersonal sources of information. Professional sources are used as legitimizing influences with commercial sources of little use. Reference groups and their opinion leaders are the factor with most influence with the later adopters. We can see from this scant information that sales personnel will not be an effective force in the first part of product introduction. The general-interest magazine would not be as good a media source as the professional or accepted trade journal. We will cover media selection and mass communication in detail when we deal with promotion problems.

Consumer Behaviour Models

Analyzing consumer behaviour through reference group theory, as we did in the last section, leaves one critical area undiscussed. It is important to have some understanding of the basic psychological and emotional needs we try to satisfy in our individual and group behaviour. Research has separated out a group of psychological needs that affect marketing decisions. We will review this area very quickly. Next we will draw on several theories of consumer behaviour to develop a single set of behavioural models. We will end this chapter with a review of current techniques used in the analysis and prediction of consumer behaviour.

Psychological and Emotional Needs

One author claims that the various lists of psychogenic needs can be put into the following three groups:
"1. Affectional needs—the needs to form and maintain warm, harmonious and emotionally satisfying relations with others.
2. Ego-bolstering needs—The needs to enhance or promote the personality; to achieve; to gain prestige and recognition; to satisfy the ego through domination of others.
3. Ego-defensive needs—The needs to protect the personality; to avoid physical and psychological harm; to avoid ridicule and 'loss of face'; to prevent loss of prestige; to avoid or to obtain relief from anxiety."[21]

---

[21] Bayton, James, "Motivation, Cognition, Learning—Basic Factors in Consumer Behaviour", in Bliss, *Marketing and the Behavioural Sciences*, Allyn & Bacon, Boston, 1963, p. 46.

The older classical psychologists, when forced to reduce their lists of basic needs, usually mentioned: security, recognition, response from others and new experience. E. Jerome McCarthy in his book, *Marketing; A Managerial Approach,* lists eight emotional purchase motives that are of importance to marketing management.

"1. Satisfaction of senses
2. Preservation of species
3. Fear
4. Rest and recreation
5. Pride
6. Sociability
7. Striving
8. Curiosity."[22]

Berelson and Steiner, in an example of a long list of learned motivation, classify twenty-eight basic psychogenic needs. Examples from this list are presented to convey the full scope of the problem facing marketing managers who want to understand consumer behaviour.

"● Need Acquisition (Acquisitive Attitude). To gain possessions and property. To grasp, snatch or steal things. To bargain or gamble. To work for money or goods.

● Need Conservance (Conserving attitude). To collect, repair, clean and preserve things. To protect against damage.

● Need Order (Orderly attitude). To arrange, organize, put away objects. To be tidy and clean. To be scrupulously precise.

● Need Retention (Retentive attitude). To retain possession of things. To refuse to give or lend. To hoard. To be frugal, economical and miserly.

● Need Construction (Constructive attitude). To organize and build."[23]

Consumer behaviour patterns are shaped by various combinations of many needs. No single product could hope to appeal to personalities formed by each of these needs. What is important is that the marketing manager recognize the needs his product can fill and to direct his promotional effort towards the population that has these needs. Any other arrangement neglects the basic tenets of the marketing concept.

Models of Consumer Behaviour

"Consumers are rational decision makers." That is how we started this discussion of consumer behaviour. We will now

---

[22] McCarthy, E. Jerome, *Basic Marketing; A Managerial Approach,* Richard D. Irwin Inc., Homewood, Ill., revised 1964, pp. 241-242.
[23] Berelson, op. cit., p. 257

expand the concept to include problem solving in consumer behaviour. Alderson puts the concept this way: "rational problem solving is a key aspect of consumer behaviour. . . . Both habit and impulse are undeniably important in a comprehensive view of consumer behaviour. Both, however, play their part within a broader pattern of adaptation which cannot be explained by either. Rational decisions and rational planning are as vital to the household as to the business firm."[24]

What problem is the consumer concerned with solving? From a heterogeneous assortment of goods on the store shelf, the consumer must select and build an optimal assortment of goods to meet present and future demands. With a limited supply of time and money the consumer must build an assortment of goods to meet an uncertain demand. We might reduce the consumer's choice problem to the level of a business decision under uncertainty or risk.

Alderson states the uncertainty problem in the following manner: ". . . To reduce uncertainty to the point where a course of action can be adopted with some confidence . . . The problem solver is trying to see the essential structure of a complicated situation and trying to make the best gamble in being prepared for future requirements."[25] If these statements are true, we can gain insight into consumer behaviour from decision theory.

William S. Peters, in an article entitled "Utility Uncertainty and the Consumer-Buyer", reviews decision theory in relation to consumer buying.[26] We will look at some of his more important points. Peters makes a strong point of showing that the marginal utility of money is not linear. "Excepting the historical viewpoint of constantly diminishing marginal utility of money, the descriptions of choice behaviour under differential risk discussed thus far find general agreement in observed preference of low probability of large gain. However, three alternative explanations of this behaviour have appeared:

1) increasing marginal utility of large money gains,
2) persistent over-estimates of the frequency of winning at long odds and
3) psychological over-estimates of personal chances of winning."[27]

24 Alderson, *Marketing Behaviour,* op. cit., pp. 164-165.
25 Ibid., p. 167.
26 Peters, "Utility, Uncertainty, and the Consumer Buyer", in Cox, Alderson, Shapiro, *Theory in Marketing,* Richard D. Irwin Inc., Homewood, Ill., 1964, pp. 254-267.
27 Ibid., p. 257.

While these three statements assume a knowledge of probabilities, they do help us in looking at a consumer who has no explicit knowledge of the probabilities of success in the decision being made.

The overly extravagant nature of certain advertising claims plays on consumers, attaching high utility to a large gain without regard to the probability. Consumer thinking may follow the line that, by using X hair tonic, it will make him an irresistible male, and who can afford to miss that chance?

Peters makes a plea for more research into the area of probability and consumer choice. He points out that studies have shown probability estimates and utility change with age and sex. Other studies show that behaviour towards risk changes with occupation, social class and reference groups. If consumer behaviour can be reduced to statements of probability when faced with uncertainty or risk, then the marketing manager is in a much stronger position.

Howard, in *Marketing Management; Analysis and Planning,* presents a series of analogues that describe consumer purchasing behaviour under conditions of Extensive Problem Solving (E.P.S.), Limited Problem Solving (L.P.S.) and Automatic Response Behaviour (A.R.B.).[28] His purpose is to describe how a customer moves through the decision process. According to Howard, five basic factors vary within each of the three stages of problem solving: (1) the probability of repeating previous response, (2) latency of response or the amount of time from triggering of a cue to response, (3) amount of ideation or the amount of cognition, (4) nature and number of stimuli affecting behaviour, and (5) number of alternatives considered.

Under conditions of E.P.S., there is a low probability of repeat purchase, there is considerable ideation, a large number of stimuli are perceived and many alternatives are considered. To the marketer, this means that the chances of a customer repeating a purchase are low. Before the customer makes the purchase, there is a good deal of conscious thinking. Many stimuli are perceived, which means that your product is not necessarily the only item being considered. There are typically many alternatives being evaluated at the same time.

As a customer moves into a condition of Limited Problem Solving, the probability of his repeating a purchase increases. He thinks less about the purchase, fewer stimuli are perceived

---

28 Howard, *Marketing Management; Analysis and Planning,* Richard D. Irwin Inc., Homewood, Ill., 1963, pp. 31-112.

and fewer alternatives are considered. Marketers are trying to get customers into a condition of A.R.B. At this point the consumer is assumed to stop learning and his purchase decision becomes instantaneous. The customer perceives his desire and, with no ideation or evaluation of alternatives, he chooses the same product he purchased the last time.

Howard's model of consumer behaviour is based on the central concepts of learning: drives, cues, response and reinforcement. These four concepts lead to the behavioural equation $B = P \times D \times K \times V$.[29] B is equivalent to response or, in laymen's terms, it is when the customer purchases a product. This purchase decision, according to the behavioural equation, is determined by the multiplied force of P, D, K and V. P is a person's predisposition. It represents how strongly a person is predisposed towards purchasing a particular item. It is predisposition that changes most radically as a person moves from E.P.S. to A.R.B. D represents what is formally called drive level. It is basically how much he desires or how badly he wants to satisfy a particular drive. K is the amount of incentive there is to satisfy the drive. One may be exceedingly hungry but he does not have any incentive to eat because his mouth is swollen from a recent visit to the dentist. A person must have both drive and incentive before he will act. Finally, V represents how strongly a particular cue is perceived. The cue is the event or picture that triggers the desire to purchase or act. For B or a particular act to take place, P, D, K and V must all have a positive value. In other words, if a person lacks any one of predisposition, drive, incentive or cue, he will not purchase.

For a complete discussion of how the actual choice process or purchase decision takes place, you are referred to Howard. The following is a list of some of the factors that will affect a person in his purchase decision:
1. The triggering cue.
2. Personal and impersonal information.
3. The quality, availability, service, price and number of alternatives.
4. The amount of favourable and/or unfavourable experience the person has had with the product.
5. The level of predisposition.
6. The importance of the purchase.
7. The ease with which a decision can be evaluated.

---

29 Ibid., p. 43.

8. The amount of time allowed to make the decision.
9. Financial status of the buyer.
10. Culture.
11. Social class.

This list is by no means complete; it should simply serve as a guide to the types of factors which must be considered in making a marketing decision. As people move from E.P.S. to A.R.B., the amount that each of the above factors will affect his behaviour changes. This relationship between factors and a customer's behaviour must be learned for successful marketing management.

Motivation Research

Information about consumers can be divided into two categories: quantitative and qualitative. Both types of information are important for making marketing decisions. It is usually fair to say that quantitative information is easier to obtain than qualitative. We can usually find out the age, sex, education level and race characteristics of a population from secondary sources or relatively simple questionnaires. Characteristics such as "how many" or "what proportion" are slightly harder to get answers to but present no insurmountable problems. The question that asks "why" or "would you?", and calls for a qualitative evaluation, can cause serious trouble for the market analyst.

Our discussion of consumer behaviour was primarily concerned with why people act as they do. The need for information in this area is acute and, as a result, a set of research techniques known as motivation research has evolved. Motivation research has two developed definitions. One says that it is the technique used to establish the motives of an individual in a specific case by the use of indirect methods. The second technique or definition claims to establish motivation through the respondent's own explanation. For our purpose, we will claim motivation research to be the technique used to uncover true motivation.

One of the first people to apply the knowledge that people will not always respond honestly to a questionnaire was Elmer Roper. To overcome problems of personal bias or ego involvement in answers to direct questions, Roper developed what could be called the Oblique Question Technique. For example, when Roper wanted to analyse attitudes towards a power company he asked people if they felt their electricity bill was

39

too high. In another case, Roper had to locate army units with the most faith in their officers. Instead of a frontal attack the question asked was: "How is chow in this unit?"

Today, under the influence of clinical and social psychologists, the projection technique has been developed to gain insight into consumer behaviour. "The projective approach includes a wide variety of actual techniques, with one basic element in common. They are all essentially attention-diverting devices. Most, in addition, aid in articulation of reactions which the respondent might have difficulty describing. On their faces, none of the stimuli presented seem to call for a highly personal reaction by the respondent. They are in the form of games, or reports, on how fictitious third persons might react, or other such devices. But the responses obtained are analysed as an inferred projection of the respondent's own feelings and emotions."[30]

Examples of projective techniques would be sentence completion, thematic apperception tests, cartoon technique, word association and semantic differential tests. Sentence completion works by presenting the respondent with an incomplete sentence and asking him to complete the thought with the first words that come to his mind. The technique can be used to gain insight into personality and to determine attitudes towards a product.

Thematic apperception tests consist of the use of a picture about which respondents are asked to tell a story. The pictures will often show a person in some ambiguous situation in some way related to the product being tested. Cartoons can often be used to put people in role-playing positions. The respondent is handed a cartoon with the circle over one person's head blank. He is then asked to read the cartoon and fill in the blank. Again it is hoped that the respondent will reveal personal characteristics or motives through a third person.

Word association is a game most of us have played. You are given a word and asked to reply with the first word that comes to mind. In the market research situation, the interviewer reads a word and asks the respondent to reply within three seconds. The list of words will usually be divided between neutral, classification and critical words. Critical words are directed towards the product being tested, while classification words are used to get general information about the respondent.

"The semantic differential is essentially a combination of controlled association and scaling procedures. We provide the

[30] Wasson, *The Strategy of Marketing Research*, Appelton, Century & Crofts, New York, 1964, p. 144.

subject with a concept to be differentiated and a set of bipolar adjectival scales against which to do it, his only task being to indicate, for each item (pairing off an item with a concept) the direction of his association and its intensity in a seven-step scale. The crux of the method, of course, lies in selecting the sample of descriptive polar terms ... By semantic differentiation, then, we mean the successive allocation of a concept to a point in the multi-dimensional semantic space by selection from among a set of scaled semantic alternatives. Differences in the meaning between two concepts is then merely a function of the differences in their respective allocations within the same space."[31]

The major weakness in any type of projective technique is the involvement of a third party to analyse and qualify the results. The third person must interpret the depth of feeling involved in most of the responses and must also interpret the true meaning of many ambiguous responses. Even with these defects, projection is a valuable tool when used correctly by experts.

We have left until last the most widely known motivation research technique—the depth interview. Although there is conflict about the exact definition of a depth interview, we can generalize and say that it is a meeting between interviewer and respondent where various techniques are used to get the respondent to talk freely about a subject and hopefully to reveal his true attitude. We say hopefully because very few depth interviewers would guarantee the validity of their findings. Because depth interviews are conducted with small numbers of people, it is difficult to apply any statistical validity to their results. Perhaps the best we can expect from the depth interview is the development of a series of testable hypothesis.

Conclusion

This concludes our discussion on consumer behaviour. We have looked at the nature of human behaviour, the role of reference groups and the part that learning plays in consumer behaviour. Human motivation was reviewed and an analogue of consumer behaviour was presented. Lastly, we have quickly looked at motivation research.

Our purpose was not to make you an expert in any of the areas covered. Rather we hoped to have exposed you to relevant concepts and sensitized you to the theory of human behaviour. The ability of the marketing manager to carry out a successful marketing programme will depend heavily on the information he has about consumers.

---

[31] C. E. Osgood, G. T. Suci, and P. H. Tennenbaum, *The Measurement of Meaning*, Univ. of Illinois Press, Urbana, 1957, p. 273.

Marketing: the Management Way

DISCUSSION QUESTIONS

1. In what ways does a culture express itself and thereby affect marketing decisions?
2. Describe group influence on consumer behaviour.
3. Describe the process of new product adoption.
4. Discuss the relationship between learning theory and consumer behaviour.
5. Describe why marketing research uses projective techniques in learning about consumer behaviour.

BIBLIOGRAPHY

ALDERSON: *Marketing Behavior and Executive Action*, Richard D. Irwin Inc., Homewood, Ill., U.S.A.

America's Tastemakers, New Jersey Opinion Research Corporation, Princeton, N.J., U.S.A., 1959.

BAYTON, JAMES: "Motivation, Cognition and Learning—Basic Factors in Consumer Behavior", in BLISS: *Marketing and the Behavioral Sciences*, Allyn and Bacon, Boston, Mass., 1963.

BERELSON & STEINER: *Human Behavior, An Inventory of Scientific Findings*, Harcourt, Brace and World, New York, N.Y., U.S.A., 1964.

GRAHAM: "Class and Conservatism in the Adoption of Innovations", *Human Relations*, Vol. 14, No. 1, 1956.

HOWARD: *Marketing Management: Analysis and Planning*, Richard D. Irwin Inc., Homewood, Ill., U.S.A.

KATZ & LAZERFIELD: *Personal Influence*, New York Free Press, Glenco, New York, U.S.A., 1955.

LANSING & KISH: "Family Life Cycle as an Independent Variable", *American Sociological Review*, October 1957.

MARTINEAU: "Social Class and Spending Behavior", *Journal of Marketing*, Vol. 23, October 1958.

McCARTHY: *Basic Marketing—A Managerial Approach*, Richard D. Irwin Inc., Homewood, Ill., U.S.A.

OSGOOD, SUCI & TANNENBAUM: *The Measurement of Meaning*, University of Illinois Press, Urbana, Ill., U.S.A., 1957.

PETERS: "Utility, Uncertainty, and the Consumer Buyer", in COX, ALDERSON & SHAPIRO: *Theory in Marketing*, Richard D. Irwin Inc., Homewood, Ill., U.S.A., 1965.

TOMOTSU SHIBUTANI: "Reference Groups as Perspective", in *Marketing and the Behavioral Sciences,* Allyn and Bacon, Boston, Mass., U.S.A., 1963.

WASSON: *The Strategy of Marketing Research*, Appelton Century Crofts, New York, N.Y., U.S.A., 1964.

ZALTMAN: *Marketing, Contributions from the Behavioral Sciences*, Harcourt, Brace and World, New York, N.Y., U.S.A., 1965.

levels. What general management sees as a tactic is often broad enough to serve as a strategy for lower levels of management. The total amount of capital allocated to the marketing department in the corporate budget is a general management tactic. This same budget allowance becomes one of the restraining variables in the marketing department's statement of goals, objectives and policies.

Planning and control are usually treated as separate subjects in management courses. We will also follow this procedure, but with one qualification. At the end of Brian Scott's definition we would add the following thought: Planning, to be complete, must include a device to stimulate replanning when initial plans are not being met or the planning environment changes.

Long-Range Planning: Definition

We have mentioned that scope and time are the basic factors in defining or classifying a plan. Time is the usual variable in differentiating between long- and short-range plans. The time concept we are talking about is not how long from now we will make a decision, but how far into the future our current decisions will govern behaviour. Drucker has expressed this idea as follows: "The next thing to be said about what long-range planning is not, is that it does not deal with future decisions. It deals with the futurity of present decisions. Decisions exist only in the present. The question that faces the long-range planner is not what we should do tomorrow. It is what do we have to do today to be ready for an uncertain tomorrow."[3]

Scott develops four concepts of time which he feels are relevant to the futurity of current decisions. "The first of these is the 'plan preparation time'. A plan which requires collaborative activity and the gathering of information which is not readily available may take months to complete; a simple plan with facts readily available may take only minutes. Second, there is the necessary lead time which the plan requires for implementation. Lead time is a measure of the time which must elapse following one occurrence before a subsequent occurrence can take place. The third concept measures the direct impact time of the planned activity, which is the period of time during which the activity now planned will continue to operate or to have direct influence on operations. Finally, there

---

3 Drucker, "Long Range Planning" in *Management Science,* Vol. 5, April, 1959, p. 239.

is the measurement of epochal time. This requires assessing historic trends and changes in order to determine the types of considerations which are likely to become of great importance to future business generations. It does not strive to measure futurity in any precise manner, but it suggests the kinds of momentous changes which may take place during coming decades."[4]

The Drucker article on long-range planning starts off by defining what long-range planning is not. It would pay to review these thoughts. First, Drucker says long-range planning is not forecasting. He says that L.R.P. is necessary because we cannot forecast. Also, forecasting is an attempt to calculate future probabilities, while L.R.P. is concerned with changing these probabilities. We have already covered Drucker's second point that L.R.P. does not deal with future decisions. As his third and final point Drucker says L.R.P. is not an attempt to eliminate or minimize risk. Rather it is an attempt to choose the proper risk to take.[5]

Drucker very carefully avoids placing a specific time value on long-range planning. While the futurity of present decisions is covered in his definition, it is basically the type or scope of the decision that makes it long-range. "It is the continuous process of making present entrepreneurial (risk-taking) decisions systematically and with the best possible knowledge of their futurity, organizing systematically the efforts needed to carry out these decisions, and measuring the results of these decisions against the expectations through organized, systematic feedback."[6]

Scott also refuses to answer the question of how long is long-range: "The fact is, however, that this whole question of 'How long is long-range?' cannot be answered specifically. Circumstances vary from case to case, and the significance of the time variable becomes apparent only when it is associated with the scope and the subject matter of the plans being contemplated."[7]

Why Plan?

To the management student, the need for planning is often accepted without much thought. We should properly ask ourselves if planning is necessary. Many companies seem to get

---

4 Scott, op. cit., pp. 30-31.
5 Drucker, op. cit., pp. 238-240.
6 Ibid., p. 239.
7 Scott, op. cit.

along quite well with no formal planning procedure. The success of one operation leads directly into the next. In some smaller companies that are dominated by one-man rule, there is no formalized planning. While these examples exist, they are by no means a justification for not planning. Planning is necessary for that point in time when momentum and a strong leader are not sufficient enough to manage a firm.

The single most important factor in creating a need for planning is change and the uncertainty created by change. Even if the future were certain, we would have to plan to cope with changes we fully expect. Under conditions of certainty, planning would reduce to a co-ordinating function but planning would still be necessary.

It is often argued that the basic uncertainty of change makes planning impossible. But the businessman must make some assumptions about the future and, through planning, he must anticipate changes which will change these assumptions. Change itself is of two natures: continuous or discontinuous. Continuous changes are the results of a smooth progression in technology or a continuation of basic trends. Discontinuous change represents a complete break in the linearity of a progression. It is the giant step forward, the major scientific breakthrough. It is the type of change that must be most fully prepared for and which requires the most planning.

While the manager cannot and should not try to predict the exact timing of a discontinuous change, his planning staff should be preparing for its eventuating.

The product life-cycle which we covered in an earlier discussion creates a basic need for planning. If long-range planning has been effective, the transition from one product's life cycle into the life cycle of a new product will be smooth and will take place at the company's convenience. There will not be a need for expensive crash programmes to develop new skills and technology.

Planning also serves a purpose by focusing attention on enterprise objectives. Because planning requires a co-ordinated structure, management must keep everyone working towards a consistent set of objectives. Planning will give management the opportunity to continuously re-evaluate its objectives.

Planning serves a truly economic function by preventing suboptimization. Without the co-ordination required by planning, individual units may optimize their operation to the detriment of the entire company

Finally, planning is an essential for control. Without plan-

47

ning, management cannot evaluate its performance and without evaluation there can be no control.

Marketing and Long-Range Planning

In our first discussion of "The Nature and Scope of Marketing Management", we listed ten criteria to be met by a firm if it was to be considered customer oriented. It would pay to repeat the second and third criteria.

"2. It is assumed that marketing activity which serves consumer's needs can be planned, and corporate destinies shaped to a large extent, by planned marketing effort.

3. Short- and long-range planning of company activities on a continuing basis, and the development of consistent strategies and tactics resulting in an integrated system of marketing action, are seen as the key to marketing management's task."

The steps involved in long-range planning are the same for general management and marketing management. The discussion that follows will deal with some of the overall problems of long-range planning, but it is equally pertinent to the problems of long-range planning in marketing.

The Planning Process

Most authors agree that there are five steps in the planning process:

(1) establishing objectives,
(2) establishing planning assumptions or premises,
(3) searching for facts and alternative courses of action,
(4) evaluating courses of action,
(5) selecting a course (or courses) of action.

In print, these five steps look and sound as if there is a clear line of delineation between each of them. Nothing could be much further from the truth. The planner is almost always involved in two or three phases of the planning process at one time. Unfortunately, we can only present one step at a time. As long as one remembers this is an artificial separation, there is no great danger.

Establishing objectives begins with what Scott calls "undertaking corporate self appraisal" and marketing authors call undertaking a marketing audit. When looking at the general corporate structure, the planner must evaluate the values, predispositions, prejudices and preoccupations of top management. Evolving corporate strategy must blend with the personalities

48

of the implementing authority. On the functional marketing level, the planner would look most closely at the technical competence of the marketing staff. He would inventory the particular skills of each man on the team.

"What business are we in?" is a relevant question at all levels of management. Most companies answer this question with a product or process identification. In other words they answer, "the automobile industry or the chemical process industry". A more useful answer for long-range planners would identify the nature of the business by its end use; such as a television station defining its business as the news and entertainment industry.

If marketing management is not to stifle creative innovation, the corporate business must not be defined in terms that guarantee obsolescence. Tying a marketing team to a product or process definition will always leave the company far behind in technology and skill when a discontinuous change takes place.

Objectives are by no means the first product to evolve in the establishment of long-range plans. A final statement of objectives cannot be made until every other step in the planning process has been completed. To start his job, the planner is most often supplied with a preliminary set of objectives which are modified throughout the planning process. Each of us has had the personal experience of adjusting our objectives as we gained a clearer picture of the environment in which we were dealing. Corporate objectives or departmental objectives are no different. As corporate understanding of the environment changes, so should corporate objectives.

Planning premises are basically assumptions about future events. In decision theory terminology, these assumptions make up the various states of nature. The planner may start off with a list of factors which he feels will have bearing on the development of a long-range plan. Initially this list can be divided into three segments by degree of controllability: non-controllable, semi-controllable and controllable. Once in this form, the events can be subdivided further by introducing probability estimates about the occurrence of uncontrollable or semi-controllable events. One of the planner's more difficult jobs is deciding how much certainty is needed in making probability estimates.

At the general management level, the planner may have a limited number of assumptions about the future imposed by company presidents or boards of directors. The marketing manager will have a great many more imposed assumptions. Because of the critical nature of certain assumptions, it is necessary to have every departmental manager agree to using the same set of assumptions. If marketing and finance used different assumptions about general economic conditions, capital might or might not be available to pay for marketing plans.

The marketing manager's prime concern at this stage of the planning process should be the development of assumptions about changes in competition, technology and distribution. Anticipating and planning for changes in each of these areas will keep his product abreast of continuous changes and may provide the insight for developing a discontinuous change.

Discontinuous changes of a technological nature are the most difficult type of change for a company to cope with. Understanding the basic causes of discontinuous change can help marketing management anticipate these changes. It seems obvious that additional technological knowledge precipitates technological change, but what factors stimulate the collection of additional technological knowledge?

The research orientation of an industry will set the initial tone for technological improvement. Certain industries are notorious for the amount spent on research. The marketing manager in a research-oriented industry must appreciate that his product's life cycle is likely to be relatively short. Competitive structure will have a direct influence on the spread of technological change. Severe competition, while it should stimulate the search for differential advantage, often has the effect of restricting basic research. Finally, continuous change has an eroding effect on the relationship between labour and capital. A small technological advance may be all that is necessary to precipitate the complete rethinking of what looked like a stable process or product.

Scott sums up the planner's problem as follows: "The chance element in discoveries and inventions is usually less significant than first appearances indicate. Even though a specific technological advance may appear to be discontinuous in relation to past developments, it is usually based on an accumulation of past knowledge and achievements in the subject area. Because environmental conditions were ripe for it, the advance often appears in retrospect to have been more inevitable than accidental."[8]

---

[8] Scott, op. cit.

Market Planning

Specific search, evaluation and selection techniques employed by general management in long-range planning are beyond the scope of our discussion. We will now shift the focus of our attention to the principles of market planning with a limited amount of attention to the search, evaluation and selection process. A more complete discussion of these three phases of planning will take place when we discuss the development of market strategy and campaigns.

This would be a good time to introduce the concept of short-range planning. In short-range planning, efforts are directed toward the step-by-step execution of a strategy. This is the type of planning where objectives are stated with some degree of finality and the means for achieving them are selected.

According to Alderson and Green, the end products of market planning are systems, campaigns, facilities and organizations. "Planning in marketing has four primary end-products. The term plan is probably most readily associated with a campaign . . . but campaigns use marketing facilities which also need to be carefully planned. There is also the larger problem of production facilities which must be planned with the requirements of the market in mind. Organization is the third end-product of planning. . . . Finally it is possible to plan an entire marketing system which embraces facilities, organizations, and the procedures for using them . . .

| Systems | Mount | Campaigns | using | Facilities | and | Organisations | "[9] |

These four end-products of planning exist in an environment governed by optimizing and structural principles. The optimizing principles should help the planner make best use of his resources, while structural principles are concerned with the pattern of activity necessary to achieve optimality.

Optimal use of time should be the goal of planning a campaign. The planner is concerned with the relationship between time and the output of the campaign. "More precisely, the aim is to maximize net outputs or the excess of outputs over inputs. . . . This objective is subject to the constraints as to cost and risk."[10]

Marketing facilities are planned to make optimal use of space. The actual utilization of the space will depend on the type of

---

[9] Alderson and Green, *Planning and Problem Solving in Marketing,* Richard D. Irwin Inc., Homewood, Ill., 1964, pp. 318-319.
[10] Ibid., p. 359.

marketing facility being planned. Space would be optimized very differently in a warehouse and a retail outlet.

"The indicated goal of an organization is to optimize decision power. The measure is to make sound decisions and to make them promptly enough so that the system can adapt to the circumstances of the environment . . . the goal for a system is to optimize its operational effectiveness. In considering how this can be done, it is convenient to think of a system operating in both a horizontal and a vertical dimension. . . . The system operates in the horizontal dimension to maximize competitive adjustment. In the vertical dimension the firm seeks good co-ordination with its supplier and its customers."[11]

Alderson summarizes the Principles of Optimization in a chart similar to the following one:

CAMPAIGNS optimize use of time.
    a. maximize outputs for specified period.
    b. minimize elapsed time, subject to constraints on cost.
FACILITIES optimize use of space.
    a. minimize movement.
    b. maximize exposure.
ORGANIZATIONS optimize decision power.
    a. maximize expected value.
    b. minimize policy exceptions.
SYSTEMS optimize operational effectiveness.
    a. maximize competitive adjustment.
    b. maximize channel co-operation.[12]

Designing the structure of a campaign concerns three planning levels: sequence, duration and date. Sequences of events are determined by a principle of precession. This means you arrange the sequence of events in what seems to be a logical order, starting with the result and working back to step number one. Through sequence manipulation the final campaign duration is set. In an effort to reduce the time and cost of a campaign, the possibility of having events added, deleted or running concurrently should be examined. If possible, a date should be set for the last event and all other dates determined by working backwards. Those of you who are familiar with P.E.R.T. will see the similarity between it and campaign structuring.

Planning for facilities takes place by considering proximity, area and site in that order. Proximity will deal with the problem of maintaining smooth access to the facility. The area problem is attacked as a balancing between space needs and cost. Finally, a site must be chosen that is flexible. Facilities usually become obsolete while under construction.

Organizational planning is concerned with hierarchy, duties

---

11 Ibid., pp. 361-362.
12 Ibid., p. 362.

and personnel. Span of control and levels of control must be balanced in the hierarchy problem. The job of assigning duties within the hierarchy should be concentrated on avoiding distortion of communication. Finally, individuals must be assigned to the task.

Systems begin with statements of objectives. These objectives must balance desirable events and feasibility of achievement. A model of the system can be built and then procedures are developed for the co-ordination of the various campaigns within the system.[13]

Uncertainty and Planning

The traditional planning model does not make specific mention of uncertainty conditions. Statements of planning premises, the search for alternatives and the choice of alternatives are discussed with very little reference to probability. To complete the picture of market planning, it is necessary to discuss how uncertainty should be handled.

We mentioned earlier that when making assumptions about future events, a decision-maker could also make probability estimates about the likelihood of occurrence. With these estimates, the decision-maker can calculate the expected payoff from any decision. He would then choose the alternative with the highest expected value. This particular technique is called Bayesian Decision Making. A full description of the technique would be beyond our scope but we will review a very simple example.

We will start off with an introduction to quantitative decision theory and build up slowly to a description of the Bayesian technique. The key word a marketing manager deals with is payoff.

Decisions are most likely to be made correctly if a measure of payoff is determined. Payoff measures degree of success. Payoff should be expressed in a unit that indicates the effect to which a goal has been realized. "The use of a quantitative measure of payoff forces the decision-maker to make his decision objectively . . . on the basis of information and logic rather than hunch, feeling or emotion."[14]

Once a unit of payoff has been selected it is necessary to choose a criteria for deciding between alternative courses of

---

13 This discussion of optimizing and structural principles is based on the treatment of the subject in Alderson and Green, *Planning and Problem Solving in Marketing.*

14 Oxenfeldt, *Pricing for Marketing Executives*, Wadsworth Pub. Co., Belmont, Calif., 1961, p. 3

action with varying payoffs. For example, assume you are a marketing manager and must decide between introducing new product A or B. The amount of profit or loss incurred in either situation will be determined by the relative success or lack of success the new product shows. Success can be measured as High, Low or Negative. Assume further that you can make the following determinations: for product A, possible payoffs are $10,000, $2,500, $6,000—, for product B, possible payoffs are $5,000, $1,000 or $2,000—.

	High $	*Low* $	*Negative* $
A	10,000	2,500	6,000 —
B	5,000	1,000	2,000 —

What course of action should you take?

There are several criteria available to you in making your decision. If you are very conservative and want to minimize any possible loss, in the event everything went wrong, you would choose item B. The maximum loss you could incur would be $2,000. This is called the maximum criteria.

Another possible alternative would be to choose the product that would produce the highest average profit. In this case the average profit is $2,167 for product A and $1,334 for product B. The average is calculated by adding each possible payoff under a strategy and dividing by the number of possible payoffs. Obviously you would now choose item A.

A third possible alternative under the same assumption is the minimax regret criteria: "The minimax criteria says, suppose each possible outcome did occur. Then, under each possible state of nature the act which would have produced the largest possible payoff could have been determined. Arbitrarily call this payoff zero. If the decision-maker took some course of action other than the best, the criteria assumes that a 'regret' equal to the difference between best payoff and each inferior payoff would be suffered. The decision-maker should list the set of maximum regrets under each act and then select the act carrying the least regret of the set of maximum regrets."[15]

	High $	*Low* $	*Negative* $
A	10,000	2,500	6,000 —
B	5,000	1,000	2,000 —

---

15 Green, op. cit., p. 91.

	Regret High $	Regret Low $	Regret Negative $	Max. Regret $
A	0	0	4,000	4,000
B	5,000	1,500	0	5,000

In this case you would choose product A.

The three examples just cited assume that the decision-maker has no knowledge about the probability of each outcome. Fortunately most businessmen have some knowledge of how often an event is likely to happen. Let us assume in the above case that the decision-maker told us that the respective probabilities of High success were 20%, Low success 30%, and Negative success 50%. These probabilities can be applied to the possible payoffs and a figure called expected payoff can be calculated.

	High (p) $	Low (p) $	Negative (p) $
A	.10,000 (.2)	2,500 (.3)	6,000 — (.5)
B	5,000 (.2)	1,000 (.3)	2,000 — (.5)

	High + $	Low + $	Negative = $	E.P. $
A	2,000	750	3,000 —	250 —
B	1,000	300	1,000 —	300

Expected payoff in each case equals H + L + N. In our example, the expected payoff for item A is $250—and for item B the expected payoff is $300. If you were the decision-maker in this case you would choose to introduce item B.

One of the advantages of using probability estimates is that you can determine the value of purchasing information to reduce uncertainty. Let us take a simplified example and assume the decision is concerned with whether or not to introduce a product, "B". We will assume there are only two possible outcomes: High or Low sales with payoffs of $10,000 or —$3,000. The probability of "High" is 60% and the probability of "Low" is 40%. In matrix form this information is:

	P.H.	H.	P.L.	L.	E.P.
Introduce	.6	$10,000	.4	—$3,000	$4,800
Don't Introduce	.6	0	.4	0	0

Under these circumstances the decision-maker would choose to introduce the product. The market research manager now tells the manager that for $1,000 he can tell for certain if H or L will take place. Should the manager purchase the survey?

55

Without getting into any involved mathematics, let us see how this decision might be made. The way this problem has been stated we know that on six out of ten occasions "High" is going to occur. On the other four occasions "Low" will occur. If the manager knows beforehand that "Low" is going to occur he will choose not to introduce. When he knows "High" is going to occur he will introduce. This means that in a series of ten decisions made with perfect information the decision-maker would introduce product "B" six times. He would get a total payoff of $60,000. On the four occasions that he knew "Low" was going to happen there would be $0 payoff as no introduction would take place. In the long run the average payoff from the decision of whether or not to introduce product "B" would be $6,000.

$$\frac{\$60,000}{10} = 6,000$$

The expected payoff with perfect information is $1,200 higher than with imperfect information. $6,000 — $4,800 = $1,200. Under these circumstances the manager can afford to spend up to $1,200 to purchase perfect information.

There is a formal mathematical method to use when making this type of decision. One must resort to a formal approach as soon as the problem becomes any more complex than the simple problem described above.

To construct this problem, we must introduce the following concepts. The two survey results showing H or L sales as definitely occurring are called R_1 and R_2. If R_1 occurs, then H will occur. This is written $P(R_1/H) = 1.0$. If R_2 occurs, then L will occur. $P(R_2/L) = 1.0$. According to our original statement, there is no chance of R_2 and H or R_1 and L. $P(R_2/H) = 0$. $P(R_1/L) = 0$. We must also introduce three more terms.

Marginal Probability. These are the probabilities attached to H and L based on the information currently available.

Joint Probability. The probability of one or another events occurring is calculated as follows—$P(A)$ or $P(B) = P(A) + P(B)$.

Posterior Probability. The conditional probabilities of two events occurring. For our purposes, posterior probability is calculated by dividing joint probability by marginal probability.

These probabilities look as follows in matrix form:

	H	L	Joint Prob.	Posterior P(H/R)	Posterior P(L/R)
R₁	.6	.0	.6	1.0	0
R₂	.0	.4	.4	0	1.0

By manipulation of the posterior and marginal probabilities, the decision-maker can calculate the expected value of the decision with perfect information.

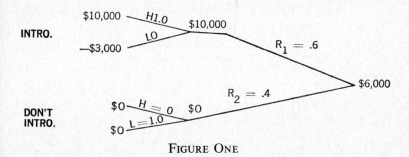

FIGURE ONE

Going back to the original example the manager compares the $6,000 expected value to the previous $4,800 and knows that perfect information is worth up to $1,200.

The above example is very unreal because very few surveys at any cost could produce 100% reliable results. In our next example we will take the same information but the survey will only guarantee 80% reliability.

Survey probabilities in this case are therefore: $P(R_1/H) = .8$, $P(R_2/L) = .8$, $P(R_1/L) = .2$, $P(R_2/H) = .2$. In matrix form the information is as follows:

	H	L	Joint	Posterior P(H/R)	Posterior P(L/R)
R₁	.48	.08	.56	.86	.14
R₂	.12	.32	.44	.27	.73
	.60	.40	100		

The calculations for posterior probabilities were:

$$P(H/R_1) = .48/.56 = .86$$
$$P(L/R_1) = .08/.56 = .14$$
$$P(H/R_2) = .12/.44 = .27$$
$$P(L/R_2) = .32/.44 = .73$$

57

Calculating the expected payoff for each possible survey result would look as follows:

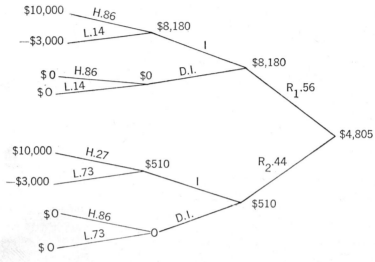

FIGURE TWO

In this case there is almost no difference in payoff with or without a survey, $4,800 as compared to $4,805, so the manager would be indifferent as to purchasing or not purchasing the survey.

Conclusions

This completes our discussion of planning and the marketing function. We have covered the broad qualitative aspects of long-range planning. A slightly more specific coverage of market planning revealed a set of optimizing principles. Finally, it was shown that quantitative decisions are possible in the planning process.

DISCUSSION QUESTIONS

1. What is meant by the word planning?
2. Describe the various types of plans that might exist within a business organization.
3. Why is planning important to marketing management?
4. What place does quantitative decision-making have in the marketing function?
5. Describe the planning process and relate it to the marketing manager's job.

BIBLIOGRAPHY

ALDERSON & GREEN: *Planning and Problem Solving in Marketing*, Richard D. Irwin Inc., Homewood, Ill., U.S.A.

ALDERSON & SHAPIRO (Ed.): *Marketing and the Computer*, Prentice-Hall, Englewood Cliffs, N.J., U.S.A.

DRUCKER: "Long Range Planning", *Management Science*, Vol. 5, 1959.

GREEN & TULL: *Research for Marketing Decisions*, Prentice-Hall, Englewood Cliffs, N.J., U.S.A., 1966.

KOONTZ & O'DONNELL: *Principles of Management*, McGraw-Hill, New York, N.Y., U.S.A.

OXENFELDT: *Pricing for Marketing Executives*, Wadsworth Publishing Co., Belmont, California, U.S.A.

SCOTT: *Long-Range Planning in American Industry*, American Management Association, U.S.A.

5

Forecasting and
Planning

THE weight of historical proof makes us listen to Drucker's warning that forecasting is sometimes a fruitless adventure. We should not accept the difficulty of forecasting as an excuse for inaction. Forecasting should not be viewed as a tool which insures the happening of a future event. Its major contribution is that it forces a systematic and careful appraisal of the past and the future.

While short-range forecasting of continuous change seems to be an easier task than long-range forecasting and the forecasting of discontinuous change, it would pay to repeat Scott's justification of long-range planning and forecasting: "The chance element in discoveries and inventions is usually less significant than first appearances indicate. Even though a specific technological advance may appear to be discontinuous in relation to past developments, it is usually based on an accumulation of past knowledge and achievement in the subject area. Because environmental conditions were ripe for it, the advance often appears in retrospect to have been more inevitable than accidental."

Our discussion will be divided into two sections. First, we will look at some of the various tyes of forecasts. We will look at general forecasting techniques used within the various forecast classifications. The second part of our discussion will be concerned with the problems of information collection. Without going into great detail, the merits of various information collection processes will be reviewed.

Types of Forecasts

Talking in broad general terms, there are three basic types of business forecasts:

(1) forecasts of general business activity,

(2) long-range sales forecasts,

(3) short-term operating forecasts.

Forecasts of general business activities are concerned with gauging changes in various economic conditions and relating these in some way to the general prosperity of the particular company. Long-range sales forecasts attempt to predict company sales over a period of years. These projections are usually for general product line rather than specific products. The long-range sales forecast is used for management decisions in the areas of plant expansion, major financing, research and executive development. A short-term operating forecast can be for periods as short as one hour or one day. They are used to regulate production, inventories, purchases, short-term cash requirements and immediate market tactics.

In the first chapter of *Business and Economic Forecasting*, Spencer, Clark and Hoguet talk about four forecasting methods;

(1) Naive,

(2) Barometric,

(3) Opinion Polling, and

(4) Econometric Methods.

We will discuss each of these methods, and look at their relative merits.

"Naive methods of forecasting may be defined as unsophisticated and unscientific projections based on guesses as mechanical extrapolations of historical data . . . typically, they are distinguished from other forecasting methods . . . in that they are essentially mechanical and are not closely integrated with relevant economic theory and statistical data."[1]

The analyst who sits down for his first look at a company's or product's future will often simply list favourable and unfavourable information about the subject under analysis. Unfortunately, many analysts stop their analysis at this point. In the simple factor-listing method, no attempt is made to quantify the relationship between favourable and unfavourable conditions. Very often there is no attempt to see if similar conditions existed in the past. Factor listing can provide valuable insight, but if it is the last step in analysis rather than the first, it will often prove a very unrewarding undertaking.

---

[1] Spencer, et al., *Business and Economic Forecasting,* Richard D. Irwin Inc., Homewood, Ill., 1961, pp. 3-4.

There is a strange power in numbers. If a thought is expressed mathematically, we often accept it as a self-evident truth. This seems to explain the widespread acceptance of simple time series and trend extrapolation as forecasting technique. The most naive type of trend extrapolation makes no attempt to analyse underlying factors. It simply says that conditions are not going to change and we can therefore simply project or forecast according to a past rate of growth or decline.

Simple trend projection makes no allowance for seasonal and cyclical variations. If one could ignore these two factors, there would still be one very major shortcoming in trend extrapolation. The most important time or period to forecast in a time series is the turning point. It is at a turning point that a company must be fully prepared. Trend extrapolation makes no allowance for picking or predicting a turning point.

Realizing that trend extrapolation left much to be desired, forecasters developed a series of barometric techniques. "Specifically, barometric methods involve the use of statistical indicators —selected time series which, when used in conjunction with one another or when combined in certain ways, provide an indication of the direction in which the economy or particular industry is leading."[2] We can talk of three types of indicators; leading, coincident and lagging. Some economic leading indicators, such as number of new incorporations, building contracts and awards, stock prices, average hours worked and orders for capital goods, are thought to change before the actual economy moves. They can therefore be used to pick the turning point. Coincident indicators change along with the trend, and lagging indicators change some time after the basic trend has changed.

Identifying leading indicators is an extremely complex task for the businessman. His choice of leading indicators will suffer the same shortcomings as those in the general economic field. The general economic leading indicators suffer from some of the following faults:

1. They are not consistent in their tendency to lead.
2. It is not always possible to distinguish between a real turn and a random wiggle.
3. The indicators only show direction of change and rarely the degree.

Some forecasters believe that the only way to find out if a series is going to change direction is to go out and interview those people whose decisions will cause changes in the series.

---

2 Ibid., p. 10.

This method of forecasting is called opinion sampling. Broad surveys dealing with capital goods expenditures have been very successful examples of opinion polling. Long-term forecasts of consumer expenditures do not seem to lend themselves to opinion polling. Executive and sales force polling are two further examples of opinion polling used in forecasting. Because of their intimate knowledge of the company and its customers, executives and salesmen are thought to have an ability to forecast business changes. If the opinions of these two groups are based simply on hunches and feelings, the forecaster should be very wary in their use. On the other hand, executives and salesmen are often in a position to get important data. It is this data and the executives' opinions which should be considered by the forecaster.

During the past decade, forecasters have come to realize the serious shortcomings of most long-term forecasting methods. With new sophistication in mathematics, statistics and data collection, a field of forecasting known as econometrics or model building has developed. These forecasting methods are based on the assumption that changes in activity can be explained by a set of relationships between variables. Combining relevant variables, each a separate series covering a past period of time, into what seems to be the best mathematical arrangements, the model builder forecasts the future on the basis of these established relationships. Multiple regression analysis is one of the model builder's more powerful tools.

Depth of Information Needed

The ability to relate variables and forecast on the basis of these relationships depends in part on the length and breadth of the available records. For example, if we were to make a one-year forecast, data from five years past might be sufficient. To complete a monthly forecast, you might still require five years' information, but it must have breadth by being in monthly format. Short-term forecasts must contain enough information to identify trends and seasonal variations. Long-term forecasts should be based on information which can show the broad effect of cyclical variation. While history is a great teacher, the fragmentary nature of past information prevents any wholesale use of very old information.

Forecasting Discontinuous Change

Economists and econometricians have a simpler task in handling discontinuous change than does the company forecaster. The emergence of radically new technology within an entire economy is easier to forecast than specific changes within specific industries. For this reason, we will look at some of the factors a long-range planner can study when trying to forecast.

"One basic reason for innovation of a new pattern of behaviour or a new operating system is that the existing system has become so overloaded that it is approaching the point of breakdown. . . . In the area of marketing facilities, this trend toward breakdown of an overload system may begin to show up presently in the supermarket where limitations on shelf space and rising pressures from manufacturers of both food and non-food products to get their products on these shelves may have to be solved eventually by drastic changes in the pattern of grocery distribution."[3]

One type of constraint that may be holding up the introduction of a broad technological improvement is the knowledge and understanding of prospective users. Recognizing areas of ignorance within industries may prove to be valuable insights into areas where seemingly discontinuous change is about to take place.

Looking at the degree of specialization within an industry may show up areas ready for radical change. Specialization is usually carried out to gain competitive advantage. There comes a point when increased specialization offers no advantage. It is at this stage that an industry is ready for radical change.

The changing relationships between costs give rise to radical change. As natural raw materials become more expensive, it does not take much insight to forecast the eventual use of a synthetic.

Galbraith's concept of countervailing power provides insight into situations when innovations will come about to correct imbalances of power. Countervailing power would describe the growth of many marketing situations.

Short-Run Forecasting

There are certain times when short-run trend extrapolation can be used as a forecasting tool. If the system being forecasted can afford a very short period of time between a turning

---

3 Green, op. cit., p. 440

point occurring and the systems forecast adjusting, then trend extrapolation is permissible. Certain types of sales forecasting and inventory control systems can afford this luxury.

The method of forecasting that holds most promise for a short-time period is trend extrapolation. A particular method of trend extrapolation that is going to gain in popularity is exponential smoothing. This technique says that the best indication of what is going to happen tomorrow is what happened today. Exponential smoothing allows you to forecast an expected range of results which are based on the inherent instability of the function being forecasted.

While the name exponential smoothing is formidable sounding, the method is simply a sophisticated technique for calculating a type of moving average. The exponential smoothing formula produces a predicted average that is the result of the previous predicted average plus or minus some amount that the previous predicted average deviated from the actual event. In formula format it looks like this:

New Forecast = Old Forecast + Alpha (actual — old forecast)

Alpha is an arbitrary figure that you pick. Its function is to determine how much weight you want to place in the previous period's results. For example, an alpha of .1 would produce a forecast that treated the material like a nineteen-time period moving average. An alpha of .5 would be equivalent to a three-time period moving average.

A short example can show this relationship quite clearly. Assume forecasted sales for January were 100 units. Actual sales were 150; what would the forecasted sales be in February with an alpha of .1 or .5?

New Forecast = Old Forecast + Alpha (actual — old forecast)
= 100 + .1 (150 — 100)
= 100 + .5 (50)

New Forecast = 105 with Alpha at .1
= 100 + .1 (150 — 100)
= 100 + .1 (50)

New Forecast = 125 with Alpha at .5

The exponential smoothing formula can be adjusted to compensate for trend and seasonal variation. A detailed treatment of this subject can be found in Brown: *Statistics for Inventory Control.*

Sources and Types of Information for Forecasting

The collection of information plays a vital role in any forecasting scheme. We will discuss several of the meanings or concepts attached to the word information. We will end our discussion of forecasting with a quick look at the various methods available for collecting information.

Concepts of Information

For purposes of our discussion, it is necessary to distinguish between two basic types of information. This is not so much a distinction in the quality or subject matter of the information, but a distinction in how the information is provided and collected. We are talking now of primary versus secondary information. We often refer to these types of information as coming from primary and secondary sources.

When someone says they are collecting secondary information, it does not mean the information is of secondary value. What he is saying is that he is going to a source that has already collected the information. For example, someone going to the latest census report to find the populations of capital cities would be going to a secondary source. The solution of most marketing problems should start with someone collecting all of the relevant secondary data. Very often in the search and analysis of secondary data you find someone else has already studied the problem and come up with a solution.

In a world changing as quickly as ours, it is impossible for anyone to keep up with the constant stream of information being published. Our most up-to-date libraries and many larger corporations have had to resort to computers for keeping track of information on any particular subject. As the field of marketing becomes subject to more and more critical analysis, the amount of secondary data available will become staggering. One thought that may deserve consideration is the formation of a marketing information library. In this library, all marketing information being published would be sorted and catalogued. Individual companies would be encouraged to contribute non-classified market research data. The time saved in searching activities could easily offset any cost of supporting this type of organization.

In contrast to secondary data, there is data collected from primary sources. This type of information collection might be called original research. When the answers to questions are not available from secondary data sources, the researcher must go to the heart of the problem for a solution. Even if information on a particular subject is published, such as the effect of smoking on cancer, other research might collect additional primary data. Unless the reliability and/or validity of a published report is doubted, there would be little sense in market researchers duplicating experiments.

This brings us to our second concept of information. A great deal of marketing information must be gathered from selected samples of large populations. In some cases there is little ability to check the validity of the information collected. Both of these problems introduce the concept of reliability of data. The statistician would say we have a problem of measuring the degree of confidence or the level of confidence attached to the data. In terms a layman can understand, once you use a sample to measure an attribute, there is a chance that the measured result is due to other factors than the attribute being measured. When going to a secondary source of information, it is important to identify what level of confidence can be attached to the data. In the collection of primary data, the collection process and the nature of the data will determine the level of confidence attached to the data collected.

Finally we must differentiate between internally and externally generated data. Very often market research is thought to deal only with data collected outside the firm. Perhaps in the strictest sense of the word, this is true. What one must be careful of is accepting any philosophy that hints marketing management does not have the responsibility for developing an internal data collection system. All too often one hears the cry that in order to satisfy the marketing manager, the company must maintain two sets of books. It is indeed unfortunate that the type of records needed to satisfy government auditors cannot satisfy management needs. The only blame that can be placed on marketing management is that for too many years they accepted useless information. There is a vast storehouse of knowledge available to marketing management, but it is often hidden behind the face of accounting figures.

External data is thought of as information other than that produced in the normal course of business. It usually requires the establishment of what might be called an intelligence-gathering function.

Sources of Information

In this section we will look at the general sources of information available to the market researcher. We will also take a look at some specific collection techniques, reviewing their relative merits.

Federal and State governments provide the largest share of secondary data available. It would be impossible to list or discuss even a small portion of these publications. Both the Federal and State governments will supply full details on all their publications.

Trade associations and professional groups are active in market research in many industries. Member firms should avail themselves of all the services provided by their trade association. If a trade association is not in the data collection business, the members should get it into the business. Trade associations are often able to collect data not available to the individual firm.

Financial reports and publications of customers and competitors often provide valuable market research data. While annual reports vary in their degree of disclosure, they usually reveal some share of the market data and give broad hints as to promotion and sales expense. Expansion plans as revealed in annual reports provide hints to new areas of sales potential.

Consumer and trade publications provide important secondary data to the company entering a new market.

Other companies who might benefit from your success should not be overlooked as a source of data. An example might be such that if you were planning to go into the manufacture of cameras, you might get valuable market data from a flash-bulb manufacturer or film manufacturers. If you are a small firm with no market research department and you purchase from a large supplier with a market research department, you should not overlook your supplier as a source of information.

Finally, one can always go to a commercial market research agency and purchase a survey or specific data.

There are many dangers involved in collecting secondary data. Information collected by others must be evaluated as to their accuracy. In general, there are eight questions you should ask before accepting someone else's presentation of "facts":

1. Under what conditions was the study made? The information should include a statement of the methods employed. There should be enough detail to enable you to build a similar survey and get similar results.

2. Has the questionnaire been well designed? Are the questions clear and unambiguous; do the questions avoid such responses that reflect prestige, embarrassment, reward or retaliation? Was the questionnaire pilot-tested?
3. Has the interviewing been adequately and reliably done? Were interviewers well trained and checked upon? Were interviewers closely supervised?
4. Has the best sampling plan been followed? What method was used to provide randomness?
5. Has the sampling plan been fully executed? Not-at-homes or refusals to answer should not be overlooked. In many cases, failure to respond amongst one group will be more prevalent than others. If this is the case, survey results are apt to be biased.
6. Is the sample large enough? The reliability of a random sample can be measured. Increasing the size of a sample will usually increase the reliability of the sample. If estimates of deviation within the population are available, it is possible to match specific sample size and level of accuracy.
7. Was there systematic control of editing, coding and tabulating?
8. Is the interpretation straightforward and logical?[4]

Before accepting secondary data at its face value, you must subject it to the same test you would expect your own research department to run on its own research.

Without going into details of procedure, let us look at the major research techniques available for collecting primary data. The most common method of collecting external data is the survey. A survey is a study intended to collect one or more items of information from a sample of respondents representative of a larger group. We will not look at panel research or motivational research techniques.

There are three major approaches open to a researcher planning a questionnaire type survey. The first is the mail survey in which questionnaires are sent to a predetermined list of potential respondents. The replies in the form of completed questionnaires are returned by mail for tabulation and analysis. The second is the telephone survey, in which a sample of respondents is reached by a telephone call. The replies to questions asked by the interviewer are recorded on a questionnaire during a phone conversation. The third is a personal

---

[4] Crisp, *Marketing Research*, McGraw-Hill Book Co., New York, 1957, pp. 173-178.

interview survey in which the interviewers ask a series of questions during a face-to-face meeting with the respondents.

Advantages of Mail Survey

1. Is usually the most economic method per completed questionnaire.
2. Easy to get widespread geographic dispersion.
3. Eliminates interviewer bias.
4. Ability to reach people with unusual work schedules.
5. Possible to get more thoughtful answers.
6. Because of anonymous answers there may be less bias due to wanting to give socially acceptable answer.
7. Sampling method is relatively simple.

Disadvantages

1. Complete lists of a universe are not usually available.
2. Answering groups may be different from non-answering groups.
3. Inability to change questions.
4. Questionnaire must be shorter and more simple than those used in personal interviews.
5. Important points cannot be pursued further.
6. Do not know who has answered questionnaire.

Advantages of Telephone Survey

1. Economy compared to personal interview.
2. Speed of getting answers.
3. Some amount of flexibility and ability to develop report.
4. Can maintain uniformity of interviewer approach through close supervision.
5. Hard-to-locate people can be reached.
6. Eliminates outside influence on respondents.
7. Some complexity allowable in questionnaire.
8. Pretesting of questionnaire is easy.
9. Lack of face-to-face relationship may allow franker discussion.
10. Sampling can be simple in populations where large proportion of people have telephones.

Disadvantages of Telephone Survey

1. True randomness rarely possible.
2. Difficulty of handling no answers or busy signals.
3. Ease with which interviewee can terminate conversation.
4. To keep "hang-ups" low, short questionnaire used.
5. Inability to gather qualitative information.

Advantages of Personal Interview

1. Only method to provide true randomness.
2. Long complex interviews possible.
3. Ability to pursue in detail.
4. Opportunity to include qualitative data.
5. Ability to use visual aids.
6. Changing sequence of questions possible.
7. Ability to precisely identify respondent.

Disadvantages of Personal Interview

1. Very high cost.
2. High degree of technical skill needed.
3. Large time requirements.
4. Interviewer problems.
5. Not-at-home problem.
6. Difficulty of reaching certain groups.
7. Some neighbourhoods not safe.
8. May be inflexible because of large expense to change questionnaire.[5]

Once a researcher decides which type of questionnaire or data collection technique he is going to use, he must then decide on a method of sampling. When all the various sampling techniques are reduced to their bare essentials, only two approaches remain, non-probability and probability sampling. Non-probability samples are the type that do not use a sampling design based on random methods with automatic selection. Because the sample is non-random and non-probabilistic, you cannot measure the sampling error.

We will concern ourselves with several different types of probability samples. The major sampling techniques are: unrestricted random sampling, area sampling and multi-stage sampling. In general, one can make the following statement about a probability sample: "With a probability sample, properly designed and executed, one can, by taking a large

[5] See Crisp, *Marketing Research*, McGraw-Hill Book Co., New York, 1957, Chapter 8, for full analysis of advantages and disadvantages.

enough sample that will be as close as desired to the results obtainable from a complete census taken under the same conditions. With a sample of moderate size, one can achieve results whose precision, in terms of range of error around the results of a complete census, can be established with confidence. The magnitude of the sampling error is determined by the design and size of the sample."[6]

Unrestricted Random Sample

In this form of sampling, the sample is drawn from the entire population. Each element in the population has an equal chance of being chosen. Selection of any one item is independent of the selection of another item. A basic application of the unrestricted random sample is to gather data for use in structuring later samples. They can be used to identify stratifications in the population which will be the basis of a later sample.

Area Sampling

Very often we do not have a complete list of all units in a population. The area sample depends on a researcher's ability to divide a physical area into units of equal size. This is usually done on the basis of a unit previously set up by the census. Once the population is divided into what we might call a series of blocks, then an unrestricted random sample is used to decide what blocks will be included in the sample. After the blocks have been chosen, lists of all possible respondents within each block are determined. From these lists, a second unrestricted sample is taken to pick actual respondents.

Multi-Stage Sampling

Area sampling, by definition, is a two-stage process. Any similar process with more than two stages would be called multi-stage.

Stratified Random Sampling

If it is possible to divide a population into mutually exclusive heterogeneous groups, stratified sampling can be used. By

6 Hansen and Horwitz, "Dependable Samples for Market Surveys", *Journal of Marketing,* National Quarterly Publication of the American Marketing Association, Vol. 24, No. 2, Oct., 1959, p. 364.

dividing a population into smaller heterogeneous groups it is possible to use a smaller sample than in the unstratified case.

Analysis of Internal Data

Perhaps the most common type of information analysis is sales analysis. It is also the most common type of market analysis produced from internal data. There are three common types of sales analysis: product, geographic and customer. Financial data also becomes an internal data source for the market analyst. Cash flow analysis and contribution to margin calculations are tools of both the market and financial analyst.

Sales Analysis

Starting with a budget as a planning device, the sales manager has many powerful tools available for sales analysis. Three basic types or classes of sales analysis exist: net sales volume, distribution cost and individual salesman analysis. Most sales analysis is a marketing management function, but the individual sales manager will have to understand the techniques if he is to control his sales force.

Sales volume analysis includes analysis of total sales volume by territory, by product and by customer classification. This type of analysis is fairly easy to complete. It involves comparing company sales on a year-by-year basis against total industry sales. Share of the market is then calculated. To prevent a problem in sub-optimization of corporate goals, profits on sales should be included in this type of analysis. What this means is, that if the company share of the market increases from 10-20% but profits fall 50%, the increased share is of little value.

Analysis of sales by territory reveals much more to a company than just looking at total sales volume. Weak territories can be pinpointed and competitive strengths and weaknesses will often be revealed.

Product analysis can be very helpful as a control device. Most multi-product firms are surprised the first time they see the large percentage of their sales that comes from only 10-20% of the product line. Analysis by product or product group permits detailed calculations of contribution to margin.

Companies that think they sell to large segments of the economy will usually find sales analysis by customers most revealing. Customers can be analysed by industry, channel of distribution or simply large accounts.

Marketing cost analysis is a detailed analysis of a firm's

distribution costs in order to find unprofitable segments of the marketing operation. Cost analysis can be used to evaluate the profitability of territories, products, classes of customers, salesmen and/or size of order. There are two schools of thought prevailing in distribution cost analysis. The first school says that the measure of profitability should be net profit; that is, total cost including direct and indirect costs are subtracted from total revenue. The other school says profit should be measured by contribution to margin. That is, total revenue is reduced by direct selling expenses, direct material and labour expenses, and any other expenses directly related to the sales. The remaining portion is contribution to margin. Sheer magnitude of the problem involved in measuring and allocating indirect marketing cost and fixed overheads makes contribution to margin a popular concept. In addition to its relative ease of calculation, contribution presents the only true picture of what happens when a product is discontinued.

A sales manager's greatest asset is his sales force. To maintain an effective team, the manager must be able to evaluate the individual members of his team. He must be able to weed out weak members for more training or replacement. There is no single measure that can be used to rate sales personnel. The best that has been devised is a composite type of review sheet.

The sales review sheet will show total sales by each salesman. It will break down the sales by product if possible. Market penetration is also placed on the review sheet. Gross margin created by each salesman can be posted. Other items to be shown are calls made per day, ratio of calls to sales, number and size of orders, direct selling expense and number of days worked. Each of the above measures should be broken into finer groups such as products and customer type when it seems further analysis is warranted.

The following example should point out the value of a salesman analysis sheet. Assume you have three salesmen, three territories, one product.

	Tom	*Harry*	*Joe*
Total Sales	$100,000	$80,000	$30,000
Potential in Territory	200,000	100,000	40,000
Penetration	50%	80%	75%
Gross Margin	10,000	16,000	4,500
Average No. of calls per day	10	5	2
Average No. of sales per day	2	.5	.25
Average Sale	$5,000	$8,000	$6,000
Selling Expense	11,000	1,600	500
Days Worked	20	20	20

If you looked at only revenue produced by salesmen you would judge Tom to be best. Analysing the sales further, you find Tom could have produced more and that on a relative and absolute basis, Harry is the best of the three salesmen.

Conclusion

Because many words have passed between the beginning and end of this chapter, we will repeat Drucker's warning: "Forecasting is sometimes a fruitless effort." There is a limit to which the various techniques and methods we have described can be pushed. If we keep these limits in mind, we are not apt to forecast beyond our ability.

DISCUSSION QUESTIONS
1. What part does forecasting play in the marketing function?
2. Analyse the various types of forecasts and show how they might be used to aid marketing management.
3. Why is trend extrapolation an unsatisfactory method of forecasting?
4. What is the value of secondary data to the marketing manager and what sources can the manager go to to collect this information?
5. Describe how internal data might be used to aid marketing management.

BIBLIOGRAPHY

ALDERSON & GREEN: *Planning and Problem Solving in Marketing*, Richard D. Irwin, Homewood, Ill., U.S.A.

CRISP: *Marketing Research*, McGraw-Hill, New York, N.Y., U.S.A., 1957.

FRANK, KUHEN and MASSEY: *Quantitative Techniques in Marketing Analysis*, Richard D. Irwin Inc., Homewood, Ill., U.S.A.

HANSEN & HORWITZ: "Dependable Samples for Market Surveys", *Journal of Marketing*, October 1959.

SPENCER et. al.: *Business and Economic Forecasting*, Richard D. Irwin Inc., Homewood, Ill., U.S.A., 1961.

STEPHEN & MCCARTHY: *Sampling Opinions*, John Wiley & Sons, New York, N.Y., U.S.A., 1958.

6

Product Planning:
Policy and Problems

WHAT specific problems create the need for product planning? Is there a general approach available for product planning? What criteria should guide product strategy? Is there an ideal organization structure for dealing with product development? These and other similar questions will provide an outline for our discussion of product planning. We will divide the discussion into two distinct parts. Part One will be a discussion of the general product planning problems. Part Two will review some of the basic quantitative decisions to be made in the process of product planning.

Justification for Product Planning

The millions of dollars being spent on product research within our modern corporations attest to the fact that new products, processes and technology are not the result of unplanned discovery. Something very important must be at stake to induce people to invest in what the averages say is a losing bet. At the most elementary level we can say that the planned and organized search for new products is a firm's only means of survival in our modern culture.

In our first discussion of the marketing function, we mentioned the need for innovation being created by political, economic, technological and sociological changes. One could actually say the need for innovation is created by the dynamic nature of culture. Later on we described the corporate drive for innovation as the search for differential

77

advantage. We are now concerned with the drives that lead to a need for product innovation and product differentiation.

We have already discussed the relationship of long-range and market planning to the uncertainty created by change. Product planning is only one part of both the corporate and market plan, yet it is a most vital link in the entire chain. The success of a long-range plan will invariably hinge on the availability of a new product to meet a new and changing consumer demand. While short-range plans are not concerned with developing new products, the success of these plans depends on how well corporate resources and products are matched to the needs of the market.

Twenty years from today, corporate profits will be generated by products most of us cannot conceive of now. While some of today's profit-makers may last for two more generations, the shelves of the supermarket, if there still are supermarkets, will be stacked with new and different products. Product planning is the activity charged with the responsibility of providing new and profitable products for management to evaluate. It is also charged with the responsibility of reviewing the profitability of current items in the product mix.

Product planning will invariably be concerned with changing the product position of the firm. By this, we mean it will be dealing with potential changes in

"(1) the kinds of goods or services offered,
(2) the number of kinds of products or different lines, that the company offers . . .
(3) the width of assortment within each product line offered,
(4) the quality level or levels that the company provides within the total range of qualities acceptable to various classes of consumers,
(5) the degree of distinctiveness."[1]

In making decisions to change product position, the product planner has five basic degrees of product change that he can call on: (1) products within the existing line can be updated so as to serve present customers better, (2) changing the product line can be accomplished by weeding out unprofitable items, (3) the current product line can be expanded to do more for current customers, (4) new products can be developed for present customers, and finally, (5) new products can be developed for new customers.

This brief discussion should have justified the need for product planning. Charles Kline, in an article in the *Harvard*

---

[1] *Marketing Handbook,* Frey Ed., Ronald Press, New York, 1965, p. 5.1.

Business Review, lists the corporate resources utilized in a product policy. The comprehensiveness of this list should serve again to point out the critical importance of proper product planning.

"*Financial Strength.* Money available or obtainable for financing research and development, plant construction, inventory, receivables, working capital and operating losses in the early stages of commercial operation.

"*Raw Material Reserves.* Ownership of, or preferential access to, natural resources, such as minerals and ores, brine deposits, natural gas, forests.

"*Physical Plant.* Manufacturing plant, research and testing facilities, warehouses, branch offices, trucks, tankers, etc.

"*Location.* Situation of plant or other physical facilities with relation to markets, raw materials or utilities.

"*Patents.* Ownership or control of a technical monopoly through patents.

"*Public Acceptance.* Brand preference, market contracts and other public support built up by successful performance in the past.

"*Specialized Experience.* Unique or uncommon knowledge of manufacturing, distribution, scientific fields or managerial techniques.

"*Personnel.* Payroll of skilled labour, salesmen, engineers or other workers with definite specialized abilities.

"*Management.* Professional skill, experience, ambition and will for growth of the company's leadership."[2]

Product Strategy and Profits

Product strategy is concerned with the overall corporate policy in relation to product introduction and deletion. We will focus our preliminary attention on the need for long-range plans dealing with introduction. We will also look at the planning procedures antecedent to developing product strategy.

The need for long-range product planning is pointed out very clearly in a recent *Journal of Marketing* article: "Time Lag in New Product Development."[3] In this article, Mr. Adler reviews the history of forty-two products. His prime concern is with the elapsed time from product ideation to market introduction. The range of time was from six months for Sinclair

---

2 Charles Kline, "The Strategy of Product Policy", *Harvard Business Review*, XXXIII, July/Aug., 1955, pp. 91-100.

3 Adler, "Time Lag in New Product Development", *Journal of Marketing*, quarterly publication of the American Marketing Association, Vol. 30, No. 1, Jan, 1966, pp. 17-21.

Power-X gasoline to fifty-five years for television. Other examples would be fifteen years for Birdseye frozen foods, Crest flouride toothpaste—ten years, Polaroid Color Pack camera—fifteen years. Some of the briefest development times were: Gerber baby foods—one year, Eversharp fountain ball-point pen—eight months. These few examples should convince you that management cannot depend on the unplanned discovery and development of new products to carry it over the tail-end of a current product's life cycle.

Product strategy must be a natural outgrowth of general corporate goals and objectives. It must also be consistent with the resource base available to the company. A type of pre-plan audit would outline the resource restrictions in developing a product strategy. This resource audit will also place the corporation in the position of having products developed that can most effectively utilize the available resource base.

The audit would begin with an analysis of tangible resources such as financial strength, nature of the manufacturing process, type of machinery being used, number and type of research personnel and facilities, size and character of the marketing organization, and the nature and type of staff services available. It is also necessary to analyse the intangible resources such as engineering skill, resourcefulness of technical personnel, flexibility and adaptability of management, the recognizable attributes by which the firm is known in the trade, and any unusual knowhow within the firm.[4]

The development of product strategy calls for a specific statement of profit and investment criteria. With the development of a profit standard, prospective product line additions can be ranked on a priority ladder. "A profitability ladder raises four questions: (1) What concept of profit is relevant? (2) What form of profit standard should be used? (3) How should profit prospects be measured? (4) What rejection level should be established?"[5]

Choosing a profit concept requires a decision between some type of incremental profit and net profit. If incremental profit is the concept utilized, all additions to or reductions in profit will be attributed to the new product. Net profit, as a concept, means that some fixed overheads are loaded onto the new product before calculating the difference between revenue and full cost. If management realizes the total commitment it makes

---

4 Staudt & Taylor, *A Managerial Introduction to Marketing*, Prentice-Hall (N.J.), 1965, p. 204
5 Joel Dean: *Managerial Economics*, Prentice-Hall, New York, 1951, p. 122.

when adding a new product, then incremental profits are a valid criteria.

In what form should incremental profits be measured, is Dean's second question. Dean suggests three possible forms: unit margins, return on investment and aggregate dollar profits. We would suggest a fourth form which is a refinement of return on investment: the discounted cash flow. This form allows you to consider the time pattern of incremental investment and revenue. We will cover an example of discounted cash flow later on in our discussion.

How much profit must a product contribute before it is included in the product mix? The idea would be to use the market cost of capital as the criteria. Deriving the cost of capital is a procedure not yet agreed upon by the experts and therefore the concept is of limited value to management. Many companies resort to the average rate of return of all current products in the mix. Another criteria would simply be that the product must contribute more than any other available alternative.

Projecting future costs and revenues as required in calculating the discounted cash flow is extremely risky. Later on in our discussion we will show how to combine the concepts of income and cost estimates with Bayesian Decision Theory.

As we know, profits are not the only criteria management uses in making decisions. The product strategy decision will often consider the following: "(1) Interrelation of demand characteristics with the existing product line. (2) Use of the company's distinctive know-how. (3) Use of common production facilities. (4) Use of common distribution channels. (5) Use of common raw material. (6) Benefits to existing products."[6]

After considering the general corporate goals and objectives, the time pattern of product life within the industry, the tangible and intangible resources of the firm and developing a profit criteria, the product planner can make a preliminary statement of product policy. This policy should include some statement about review of the current product line. We will spend some time on methods of evaluating current products and the product line.

---

[6] Ibid., p. 127.

Evaluating Existing Products and Product Lines

There seem to be several criteria a product planner can utilize when reviewing his company's product line. They are: (1) Profitability, (2) Scope of product line, (3) Marketing efficiency, (4) Production efficiency, (5) Cost, (6) Price, (7) Value, (8) Quality, (9) Service, and (10) Competition.[7]

The type of questions a product planner would ask when evaluating profitability are: Does the product line meet the corporate profit criteria? How does it compare to the average product line's profitability? How does it compare to the industry's average profit? After going through the next nine criteria, we will take a hard look at profit measurements with particular attention to the role of contribution to margin.

If a product fails the company's profitability tests, are there any real reasons for maintaining its sale? The most frequent explanation given for carrying an unprofitable item in a line is that of maintaining an image or position with distributors, dealers or customers. This explanation must come under regular critical re-evaluation. In certain cases, it will be necessary to maintain an item or complete product line. In more cases, honest appraisal will show deletion of the item to be more profitable. If maintaining a currently unprofitable line is thought to be necessary, a time limit should be set on making the item profitable or finding a convenient way to drop the item.

Certain products and product lines may be candidates for deletion or change if they create problems in marketing efficiency. Questions such as: Does the product cause special problems in handling, shipping and storage? Can normal trade channels handle the product in its current size, shape and packaging material? Does the product line require inefficient use of sales resources?

In addition to being efficient to market, a product must also be efficient to produce. No matter how important the marketing concept says it is to make a particular product, the product must fit in with the company's production ability.

When talking about evaluating a product or product line for cost factors, we are not referring to another type of profit analysis. First, the design costs of an item can be studied. This refers to value analysis. Is the amount of money being spent on components for a particular product really necessary? The goal of design evaluation is to reduce cost without reducing

---

7 D'Orsey: "Criteria for Evaluating Existing Products and Product Lines", *A.M.A. Management Report 32*, A.M.A. 1959, p. 92.

value in the customer's eyes. Secondly, manufacturing cost of a product should come under review. One of the best ways to check if your manufacturing costs are too high is to ask for outside bids.

The evaluation of price requires looking at four specific points. First, the product's price should be tested for its profit yield. If items within a product line have been priced to fit some formula for differentials between products, this formula should not be followed if the profit yield on an item can be increased with a different price. Before breaking a pricing formula, the evaluator must be sure he is not creating a problem in sub-optimizing of product-line profits.

Pricing formulas based on cost must be evaluated to insure that the price is sound from a marketing standpoint. The changing pattern of price and patent protection must be continuously re-evaluated. Finally, situations to become the price leader should be sought aggressively.

Value analysis is frequently concerned with reducing the cost of manufacturing an item. Very often, changing positions with the customer and looking at a product and how its value can be increased is a profitable undertaking. Usually, small low-cost improvements in a product contribute disproportionate value for the customer

Every product should be evaluated from a quality criteria. A product should stand up to the manufacturer's quality requirement, the customer's quality requirements and also the quality of competition's product. Quality considerations lead directly into service requirement considerations. Auditing the service requirements of a product necessitates looking at service facility needed, parts inventory and training of servicemen. Changes in a product line may be designed to reduce service overhead.

Finally, it is always wise to review the competitive situation for a product line. How does the product compare on a quality and price basis with competition? Are customers evaluating you and competition in a manner consistent with the true differences in price and quality?

Product-line evaluation refocuses corporate attention to the criteria that will affect product profits. Because critical self-evaluation is difficult, the evaluation of a product line should be formalized and in some cases it should be done by a disinterested party.

How does one decide if the profit contribution of a product is sufficient to warrant its maintainence in the product line?

Older accounting techniques would tell you to calculate total sales for the product and then subtract total costs associated with producing and selling the product. In total cost, the accountant would include arbitrarily assigned fixed overheads. The entire company product mix would then be analysed and any item showing a loss or low profit would be a candidate for exclusion.

The more modern method and one that seems to produce a more meaningful answer is the calculation of incremental profit or contribution to margin. The steps involved in identifying items for deletion are:

1. Calculate total sales for each product for a meaningful time period. This would usually be one year.
2. From total sales subtract appropriate cost figures which would include the following:
   a. Direct material costs, which includes all those raw materials necessary to complete the product.
   b. Direct labour costs including all labour necessary to produce the finished product.
   c. Variable overhead, consisting of variable factory costs such as indirect labour, and supplies which bear a direct relationship to the volume of the product produced.
   d. Marketing costs that can be directly identified to the product.
3. List all the products in the product line according to their contribution to margin.

Contribution to margin cannot be the sole criterion for inclusion or exclusion of a particular product but it is a reasonable starting point for evaluation. The futurity of the current profit must also be considered. We will cover this in more detail when we deal with discounted cash flows.

New Product Development

The addition of new products to a product line through merger and acquisition present unique problems beyond the scope of our discussion. Our concern in this section will be with the internal development of new products. We will look at the general steps in new product development and the type of organization necessary for pursuing product development. Finally, we will start our introduction of quantitative methods with a discussion of evaluation and control of new product introduction.

"The new product process can be broken down into manageable stages for planning and control. Study of case histories reveals there are six clear stages . . .

"EXPLORATION: The search for product ideas to meet company objectives.

"SCREENING: A quick analysis to determine which ideas are pertinent and should be given careful investigation.

"BUSINESS ANALYSIS: The expansion of the idea through creative analysis, into a concrete business recommendation including product features and a programme.

"DEVELOPMENT: Turning the idea-on-paper into a product-in-hand, producible and demonstrable.

"TESTING: The commercial experiments necessary to verify earlier business judgements.

"COMMERCIALIZATION: Launching the product in full-scale production and sale, committing the company's reputation and resources."[8]

While overall industry statistics show 80% of all new product introductions as failures, the Booze, Allen and Hamilton survey shows that firms with well-organized product planning programmes had a 40-50% failure rate. There seem to be certain steps that can be taken within each of the product development stages that lead towards more successful commercialization.

Booze, Allen and Hamilton present a very complete outline of the steps to be followed in developing or bringing a product to market.[9] The following is a summary outline of their suggested procedure.

"A. *Exploration*
1. Determine the product fields of interest to the company.
2. Establish a programme for planned idea generation.
3. Collect ideas through an organized network.

B. *Screening*
1. Expand each idea into a full product concept.
2. Collect facts and opinions, which are quickly available, bearing on the product idea as a business proposition.
3. Appraise each idea for its potential value to the company.

C. *Business Analysis*
1. Appoint persons responsible for further study of each idea.
2. Determine the desirable market features for the product and its feasibility.
3. Develop specifications and establish a definite programme for the product.

---

[8] *Management of New Products*, Booze, Allen, Hamilton Inc., 1960, pp. 8-18.
[9] Ibid., pp. 8-18.

D. *Development*
1. Establish development projects for each project.
2. Build product to designated or revised specifications.
3. Complete laboratory evaluation and release for testing.
E. *Testing*
1. Plan commercial experiments necessary to test and verify earlier judgement of the product.
2. Conduct in-use production and market testing.
3. Make final product decision; freeze design.
F. *Commercialization*
1. Complete final plans for production and marketing.
2. Initiate co-ordinated production and selling programmes.
3. Check results . . ."[10]

The specific organizational structure a company chooses for the development of new products should be tailored to meet the company's unique requirements. There is no single structure applicable to a broad group of companies. One general organizational requirement does seem to be somewhat universal in its application. Someone within the organization must be charged with the responsibility to co-ordinate the search for new products. This person must have the authority to oversee the entire product development procedure and it should be his responsibility to insure that the process is carried out in the manner best suited to his company's needs. The *ad hoc* appointment of different people to guide product development as the need arises, while very popular, does not allow for the specialization of managerial talent that is necessary in product development.

Quantitative Analysis

Once all of the qualitative factors in a product introduction problem have been evaluated, the final decision should become a quantitative analysis of the investment opportunity. The basic information needed in a capital budgeting problem, and new product introduction is a capital budgeting problem, is: (1) the amount of capital required, (2) the change in cash flow as a result of the project, (3) the timing of inflow and outflow of funds, and (4) the expected life of the project.

Let us take a quick look at each of these information requirements. For a complete discussion see: Hunt, Williams and Donaldson, *Basic Business Finance* (Richard D. Irwin Pub., Homewood, Ill.), 1961, pp. 612-632. The investment requirement is the cash outlay for any new equipment, plus

---

10 Ibid., pp. 8-18.

any other permanent additions to the amount of working capital required, created by the introduction of that specific product. The proper terminology would be to say we needed an estimate of the incremental capital requirement. That is the difference in capital requirements specifically created by the new investment. It is also necessary to estimate the scrap value of any depreciable assets involved in the investment.

Calculating change in cash flow is a difficult and crucial part of investment analysis. The necessary figure is an estimate of the difference between what total funds received by the business would be if the firm does not introduce the new product and what the firm is expected to receive if the product is introduced.

Because money has a time value, it is important to know the timing of all inflows and outflows of funds. Incremental income generated by a new product may be evenly spread over ten years, but the moneys received in year two are worth more at the end of the project than the moneys received in year eight.

Finally, the expected life of the new product is estimated. It is critical to have a specific time period in which a project must justify itself.

With these four pieces of information, management must now calculate if the particular investment meets a prestated cut-off criteria. The cut-off criteria will be expressed as a rate of return and is called the discounting factor.

For demonstration purposes, assume the following information. It has been suggested by the product planning committee that product X be introduced. Product X will generate an incremental cash flow of $4,000, $5,000, $6,000, $5,000 and $4,000 over the product's five-year life. To produce product X will require an initial outlay of $10,000 for machinery to be paid on installation. At the end of the machinery's second year of operation, a second payment of $4,000 must be made. Product X will also add a $1,000 per year inventory. It is assumed that the machinery has no scrap value at the end of year five. In the past, the company has averaged a 10% return on investment based on a discounted cash flow analysis. Should the company produce product X?

Year	Flows	10% Factor	Present Value
0	—10,000	1.000	—10,000
1	—1,000	.909	909
2	—5,000	.826	4,130
3	—1,000	.751	751
4	—1,000	.683	683
5	—1,000	.621	621
TOTAL INVESTMENT	—19,000		—17,094
1	$4,000	.909	3,636
2	$6,000	.826	4,956
3	$6,000	.751	4,506
4	$5,000	.683	4,098
5	$4,000	.621	2,484
TOTAL CASH FLOW	$25,000		19,680

As long as the present value of the cash flow is equal to or greater than the present value of the investment, the project should get the go-ahead. In cases where there is a limited amount of capital and an excess of investment opportunities, a very simple decision tool exists. Present value of the investment is divided into the present value of the cash flow. The resulting ratios are ranked and investments are chosen from the top of the list as capital becomes available.

Our last example made no statement about the probability associated with the cash flows generated. It is possible to apply Bayesian statistics to the capital budgeting decision. Expected cash flows are calculated with reference to some future set of events. Under varying assumptions, it would be possible to assign probabilities to these assumptions and calculate the expected value of the discounted cash flow. Returning to our example, assume that the cash flow of $19,680 was based on an assumption of HIGH SALES. Make a further assumption that there is a 20% chance of low sales, and with low sales the discounted cash flow will be $10,000. Should the company still introduce product X?

	(P) High Sales	Cash Flow	(P) Low Sales	Cash Flow	E.P.
Intro.	.8	$19,680	.2	$10,000	$17,744
Not	.8	0	.2	0	0

The expected value of the discounted cash flow is more than the present value of the investment, therefore the investment should be made.

88

Bayesian analysis allows other types of capital budgeting decisions to be made. The approach can be used to decide whether or not to proceed with the development of a product or should the decision be delayed until more information can be gathered. Putting off the decision to push a project into the next stage of development causes certain types of costs to be incurred. We will look at these costs and then work through an example of deciding if collecting more information is profitable.

There are generally three costs involved in delaying an investment decision. First, the present value of all future cash flows is reduced. By delaying the possible introduction of a new product, the probability of effective competition increases. Finally, there is the actual cash outlay in expense involved in conducting a survey.

Let us take a look at our hypothetical company when it delays introduction of product X for one year. The first time through we will assume that the only effect is on the present value of the investment and cash flow.

TABLE ONE — NO DELAY

Year	Invest.	Cash Flow	Difference	10% Discount Factor	Present Value
0	—10,000		—10,000	1.000	—10,000
1	—1,000	4,000	3,000	.909	2,727
2	—5,000	6,000	1,000	.826	826
3	—1,000	6,000	5,000	.751	3,755
4	—1,000	6,000	5,000	.683	3,415
5	—1,000	4,000	3,000	.621	1,863
					2,622

TABLE TWO — DELAY ONE YEAR

Year	Invest.	Cash Flow	Difference	10% Discount Factor	Present Value
0	0	0	0	1.000	0
1	—10,000	0	—10,000	.909	—9,090
2	—1,000	4,000	3,000	.826	2,478
3	—5,000	6,000	1,000	.751	751
4	—1,000	6,000	5,000	.683	3,415
5	—1,000	6,000	5,000	.621	3,105
6	—1,000	4,000	3,000	.564	1,692
					2,351

Because of the one-year delay there is a 10% reduction in the present value of the difference between investment and cash flow. The company would still introduce product X.

Now let us add a second assumption. Because competition will have more time to develop its own product, there will be a $1,000 decrease in sales during the product's third, fourth and fifth years of life.

TABLE THREE

Year	Inv.	Cash Flow	Difference	10% Factor	P.V.
0	0	0	0	1.000	
1	—10,000	0	—10,000	.909	—9,090
2	—1,000	4,000	3,000	.826	2,478
3	—5,000	5,000	0	.751	0
4	—1,000	5,000	4,000	.683	2,732
5	—1,000	5,000	4,000	.621	2,484
6	—1,000	4,000	3,000	.564	1,692
					$276

Although the present value of $276 is considerably less than the $2,622 of the original case, the company will still be earning an excess over 10%. Until the present value figure reaches a negative value, the investment satisfies a 10% criteria.

For our final example let us return to the first example we used in Bayesian analysis.

DECISION TO INTRODUCE PRODUCT B

	PH	H	PL	L	E.V.
Intro.	.6	10,000	.4	—3,000	$4,800
Don't Intro.	.6	0	.4	0	0

Let us also assume that all payoff figures represent the difference between the present value of the investment and the cash flows at the end of the product's life.

If the company elects to delay the introduction of product B for one year so that they may conduct an 80% reliable survey, the present value figures will change to $8,000 and —$4,000 for High and Low sales. We will assume these figures to reflect the effects of competition and also the effects of time. Should the company collect the information and, if so, how much should they spend on collection?

In this instance the marketing manager would find that the expected value of the decision after conducting an 80% reliable survey would be substantially less than $4,800. Therefore, the survey should not be purchased.

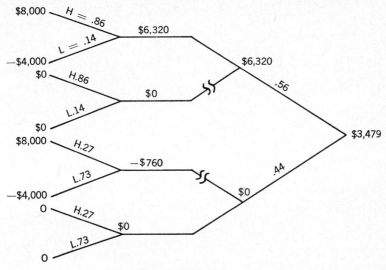

$8,000

H = .86

$6,320

L = .14

—$4,000

$6,320

$0

H.86

$0

.56

L.14

$0

$8,000

H.27

—$760

$3,479

L.73

.44

—$4,000

$0

0

H.27

$0

L.73

0

FIGURE THREE

The quantitative measures we have gone over so far help the decision-maker choose a product to introduce. Can the imposed logic of quantitative methods help the decision-maker plan and control the introduction of a specific product? Obviously, the answer is yes. The general technique known as critical path analysis provides this service.

We will assume that management's desire is to get a new product to market as quickly as possible within specified limits of cost and risk. Critical path analysis allows management to watch the relationship between time, cost and risk. It also forces management to review every step in the introduction process, to identify the process and to identify the inter-relationships of all of the various factors in introduction.

The first step in critical path analysis is the construction of an activity network. This network will show in graphic form the steps and time involved in the process or procedure being analysed. For illustration purposes, we will show a very over-simplified example. Assume product X has received preliminary management approval. All steps involved and the expected time for their completion are shown in Figure Four. Expected time is a result of applying an approximation of the normal curve formula to estimates of optimistic, normal and pessimistic completion times.

91

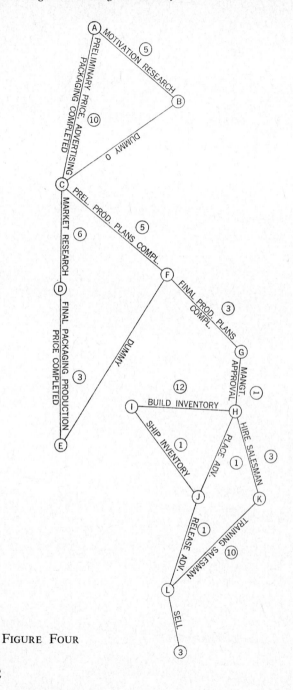

FIGURE FOUR

There are thirteen possible paths through the network **starting** at Ⓐ and ending with Ⓛ . The paths and their **completion** times are:

Ⓛ A,B,C,F,G,H,K,L,   = 27 days.

② A,B,C,F,G,H,J,K,   = 16 days.

③ A,B,C,F,G,H,I,J,L,   = 28 days.

④ A,B,C,D,E,F,G,H,I,J,L, = 31 days.

⑤ A,B,C,D,E,F,G,H,K,L, = 31 days.

⑥ A,B,C,D,E,F,G,H,J,L, = 20 days.

⑦ A,B,C,D,E,F,G,H,K,L, = 31 days.

⑧ A,C,D,E,F,G,H,I,J,L, = 37 days.

⑨ A,C,D,E,F,G,H,J,L,   = 25 days.

⑩ A,C,D,E,F,G,H,K,L,   = 32 days.

⑪ A,C,F,G,H,K,L,   = 32 days.

⑫ A,C,F,G,H,J,L,   = 21 days.

⑬ A,C,F,G,H,I,J,L,   = 33 days.

Path ⑧ , taking 37 days, is the critical path. Any attempt to reduce the amount of time the project takes must start with a reduction in some part of path ⑧ . In a more complete example, we would have shown the costs of completing each event on each path. If management had to complete the process in thirty days, they would calculate the extra cost of rushing. It is also possible to include risk estimates into the time and cost calculations.

When the number of events to co-ordinate and control gets very large, it becomes necessary to use a computer for analysis.

Manual procedures have been developed for analysing critical paths and associated costs, when the number of events being co-ordinated is in the 2-300 range.

A full critical path analysis will provide management with the following type of report. Each activity will be identified with its beginning and ending event. The expected time for the completion of each activity will be listed with a statement of optimistic and pessimistic time. Scheduled completion date and latest allowable completion is shown along with a statement of time excess or shortage usually called "slack". Estimated and actual costs can be listed and computer runs can show additional cost of compressing expected time.

We have reviewed critical path analysis so as to introduce the topic. Actual techniques and implementation can be learned from any one of the many available handbooks.

Conclusion

Our purpose has been to show you that while product planning is complex, it can be broken down into manageable sections. We have established techniques for evaluating current and future products. In the following chapters we will explore the pricing of new products, advertising, selling and distribution. These topics will be handled within the general problem areas listed.

DISCUSSION QUESTIONS

1. What factors should be studied in the marketing audit that precedes a product-planning decision and why should they be studied?
2. Describe the stages of product planning and discuss the types of decisions made at each stage.
3. What part does cash flow analysis play in product planning?
4. What information should be collected in the marketing research stages of a product development project?
5. Analyse how product planning decisions might affect corporate departments other than the marketing department.

BIBLIOGRAPHY

BERG & SCHUCHMAN: *Product Strategy and Management*, Holt, Rinehart and Winston, New York, N.Y., U.S.A.

DEAN: *Managerial Economics*, Prentice-Hall, Englewood Cliffs, N.J., U.S.A.

D'ORSEY: *Criteria for Evaluating Existing Products and Product Lines*, A.M.A. Management Report 32, A.M.A., 1959.

FREY (Ed.): *Marketing Handbook*, Ronald Press, New York, N.Y., U.S.A.

HUNT, WILLIAMS, DONALDSON: *Basic Business Finance*, Richard D. Irwin Inc., Homewood, Ill., U.S.A.

KLINE, CHARLES: "The Strategy of Product Policy", *Harvard Business Review*, XXXIII, July/Aug., 1955.

Management of New Products, Booze, Allen, Hamilton, New York, N.Y., U.S.A., 1960.

STAUT & TAYLOR: *A Managerial Introduction to Marketing*, Prentice-Hall, Englewood Cliffs, N.J., U.S.A., 1965.

7

The Pricing Decision

AFTER reading his first economics text, the marketing management student may wonder why he has to study pricing and pricing problems. All that is necessary, according to his economics text, is to find the price at which marginal revenue equals marginal costs and profits are automatically optimized. The first part of our discussion will look at the reasons why pricing decisions are not as easy to make as they might appear. We will analyse the variety of factors affecting the pricing decision. Special attention will be paid to the nature and types of costs that are relevant to this area of marketing management.

Once we have had a close look at the problems of price management, we will then analyse some of the more common pricing techniques now in fashion. With current techniques as a background, we will then develop a qualitative formula for price management. Finally, one of the newer quantitative methods of pricing will be reviewed.

Problem Areas in Pricing

Most decisions about factors in the marketing mix are made difficult by a common set of problems. Because the price decision suffers from all the common problems, in addition to its own unique set, we must review the entire range of problems with specific reference to the pricing decision.

Definition of Objectives

Managements are often faced with the problem of bringing order out of what can seem like a set of conflicting objectives.

96

If we limit ourselves to an analysis of only monetary objectives, we are avoiding at least half of the "objectives" problem. But the remaining half is complex enough to point out the price setter's problem.

Assume management states its profit objective as "to maximize profit". The decision-maker in this case must decide if price is to be used for long- or short-run profit maximization and he must develop working definitions of long and short range. Perhaps management will state its objective in terms of market-share and profit. It is not unreasonable to find that these objectives are in conflict. Again, management may state objectives in the form of rate of return on investment or even as simply as a total dollar sales figure. Within each of these objectives there is a possibility for conflicting price policies to develop. The problem of balancing the effect of various pricing strategies and multiple objectives can become a complex mathematical exercise. Often it will take a computer to choose the optimal strategy.

Identifying the Effect of Price Changes

The decision to change some portion of the marketing mix is usually based on an assumption about the changes' effect on sales or profits. Oxenfeldt tells us that this problem is insurmountable. "In plain simple fact, we rarely know . . . and we have no very good means of finding out in most cases . . . how sales would be affected by the many things that management might do to stimulate them."[1] Research can be employed to reduce the price decision from an irrational guess to a rational calculation.

Identifying the effect of price changes can be looked at in two ways. First we can be looking for the price elasticity of demand over a continuous demand curve. In simple words we want to know how much we can sell at all conceivable prices. Secondly, we can be looking for the effect of price change on a demand curve that allows for only one sale. This would be the typical competitive bidding situation. At this time we will be concerned with the first problem. We will cover bidding later in the chapter.

Correlation analysis can be used to calculate the relationship between price and sales. Simple correlation analysis between

[1] Oxenfeldt, Alfred, *Pricing and Forecasting,* reproduced by I.B.M., Poughkeepsie, N.Y., 1960, p. A-16.

historical prices and sales can be analysed if you assume your product and consumer income to have remained stable. For longer periods of time, when there are product changes or changes in income, business conditions or consumers, multiple correlation analysis is necessary.

Controlled experiments offer management the opportunity of measuring short-run price elasticity. By carefully choosing similar test markets and varying price, elasticity can be estimated. Pricing experiments can be very costly and run a high risk of unfavourable side effects from competition, dealers and consumers. For this reason, pricing experiments must be conducted with great care.

Personal interviews, questionnaires and game theory experiments may be helpful tools in testing for price elasticity. Attacks on the pricing problem from the psychological viewpoint can provide useful guidelines. Highly engineered products or capital equipment lend themselves to consumer intention surveys or consumer utility surveys.

Establishing the relationship between price and sales for any company should be done with great care and by an expert.

Uncontrollable Outside Factors

Price decisions are particularly vulnerable to the effects of outside forces. In his pricing decision, the marketing manager must include estimates of payoff under all possible conditions and states of nature. Avoiding analysis of an unpredictable variable can only lead to disaster.

Time Requirements

The pressure of time can often cause a decision to be made on an emotional basis, rather than as a rational evaluation of the alternatives. When faced with a lack of information and time, the marketing manager only hopes his intuitive decision is correct. Adequate planning in the form of contingency strategies can avoid many time-pressure problems.

Ethical and Social Problems in Pricing

The decision to raise or lower price has far-reaching political, economic, psychological and sociological implications.

Should factors outside the immediate profit situation created by a price decision be allowed to influence the decision? Are there moral implications in the selling of drugs that are not present in the selling of clothing? Should business accept a self-policing role or should all economic policing be done by the government? There are no sure answers to these questions, but the pricing executive would benefit by spending many hours thinking about his answers.

Perception and the Pricing Decision

"The field of pricing, no less than most other aspects of marketing, presents opportunities to influence customer perception. Psychological pricing, for example, is a virtual marketing speciality devoted to finding prices that seem lower than they really are. 'Sales' are almost always accompanied by a change in physical appearance of the seller's premises to create the feeling in customers that they are attending a carnival at which prizes are given away. Under such circumstances, customers apparently see different things when they look at the same price tag than they would perceive without the carnival atmosphere."[2]

Perception and perceptual bias enter the pricing picture from two avenues. First, the price-setter has his particular perception of reality. Secondly, the perceptual biases of customers determine, to a large extent, the success of any pricing decision.

In making a pricing decision, the manager usually considers the following factors: his costs, the price charged by competitors, his product's relative qualities, the response of his dealer organization to a price change, reaction of labour, government, suppliers and, most of all, customers to price changes. When armed with detailed marketing information, personal perception in variance with reality will be held to a minimum. Without detailed information the decision-maker must rely on his own perception and the perception of other members of the organization.

Oxenfeldt says that price-setters suffer from one common misperception. "It is suggested that because most price-setters exaggerate the sensitivity of the customer to modest changes in price, they may systematically charge less than the price that would provide maximum advantage to their firm."[3]

Why would price-setters tend to misperceive the sensitivity of price? Common human nature causes those who are dis-

---

2 Oxenfeldt, Shuchan, Miller & Winick, *Insights Into Pricing*, Wadsworth Publishing Co., Belmont, California, 1961, p. 66.
3 Ibid., p. 78.

satisfied with price to complain more loudly than satisfied customers. Because the price-setters hear complaints from people who usually are more discerning about price and quality, he may attribute these characteristics to all of the firm's customers. Basically, the price-setter misperceives because the information he receives is unrepresentative.

"To the extent that this misperception is widespread and strong it could be highly significant. From a broad social viewpoint, it may contribute to a desirable intensity of price competition. From the standpoint of the individual businessman, it represents a failing in employees, against which owners must guard if they would obtain maximum profits."[4]

How is it possible for a customer to misperceive price? Marketers have found that prices are not always perceived at their true value. Prices set psychologically correct, yet only one or two cents different from a price not psychologically correct, will be perceived as being vastly different. The way in which a price is perceived will vary because of the conditions surrounding the sale. When purchasing an item without making price comparisons, the customers will almost always perceive the price of items he could have bought as being equal to, or higher than the price he paid. Advertising and packaging also work to change a customer's perception of price.

Customer perception of price will often be negated along with the actual product characteristics. The product being purchased will be perceived as an image the purchaser is trying to achieve. The brand image and the customer's image of himself and his desires must be consistent. How many products are purchased without regard to cost because they impart prestige and social status to the owner?

Attitudes and Price

Attitudes as well as perception influence price from the two directions of customer and price-setter. We will look at the price-setter's attitudes first and then study how consumer attitudes affect price.

The widespread use of cost-plus pricing is good evidence that price-setters hold the attitude that price should move in parallel to costs. In the retail trades, consumer prices are usually not marked up when replacement costs first rise. The retailer holds the attitude that price should remain parallel to cost and he would not be justified in raising price until the

---

4 Ibid., p. 79.

merchandise he sells has cost him more to purchase. Government agencies help to perpetuate this attitude by only accepting the increase in costs as justification for a price increase. The concept of a fair rate of return prevails in business because of this same cost price attitude.

Customer attitudes towards price are directly related to their attitudes towards money. The importance of money is stressed from earliest childhood and for this reason most people hold very strong beliefs about the use of money. While specific individual attitudes towards money vary, it is true that these attitudes are held with much strength. The attitude of a particular customer towards money is of critical importance to the entire marketing team. Customers who fear and will go to great lengths to avoid waste will behave vastly differently from a person who views money as an expendable item. Strong attitudes towards money are best treated by adaptation of the product to satisfy the attitude rather than trying to change the attitude.

Groups, Group Behaviour and Pricing

It should go without saying that the formal and informal groups a price-setter belongs to influence his pricing decisions. An individual's allegiance to political groups within the corporation will affect his behaviour pattern. Membership in a trade association or professional group will also influence the price-setter. The price-setter's social group and its values will temper the price-setter's freedom to act in a strict, rational and economic fashion.

Up to this point our review should have made one point very clear. The pricing decision is made within a complex socio-economic atmosphere. Any statement to the effect that a pricer is capable of simply matching marginal revenue and marginal cost avoids the heart of most pricing problems. Having introduced you to the complexities of price-setting created by general management problems and behavioural science findings, we will now look at other factors affecting price; economic characteristics of the product, costs, stage of product's life cycle and finally, executive judgment.

Economic Characteristics of the Product

In review, we find the more important economic characteristics of a product fall into three groups.

101

"1. The type of product (new or old, capital goods or consumers' goods, differentiated or standardized, perishable or nonperishable, importance of style, importance of costs, original equipment or replacement).

"2. The type of firm (size, multiproduct or single product, price leader or follower).

"3. Extent of Competition."[5]

History has shown that demand is more sensitive to price in a product's early stages as opposed to the product in its later stages of life. Capital goods, utilized for the generation of profit, are insensitive to price during times of prosperity. Also, price decreases do not induce purchases during recession. Price changes have shown to be more effective in stimulating demand for consumer non-durables rather than durables. We have already discussed the reasons why differentiation creates the possibility for price competition. Product perishability, such as in food or fashion goods, reduces the control a firm has over price.

The pricing problems of a multi-product firm tend to be more complex than in a single-product firm. Cost allocation becomes almost impossible. Authority to set prices is usually delegated well down the organization structure. Many products may be carried for the expediency of having a full line.

We have already discussed the effect of industry structure and the influence of competition on pricing problems. At a later point, we will discuss the use of price to inhibit or restrict further competition.

Costs and Prices

Before we can discuss the influence of costs on price, we must clarify the cost concept. The particular cost concept used in a particular situation depends on the business decision being made. While many of the cost concepts we will be dealing with have no relationship to traditional accounts, they serve as useful tools. First, new concepts may show how useless traditional cost concepts can be. Secondly, it is important to realize that different decisions require different cost concepts.

For our purposes we will look at the following cost concepts:

1. *Opportunity* v. *Outlay Costs.*
2. *Past* v. *Future.*
3. *Short Run* v. *Long Run.*
4. *Variable* v. *Fixed.*

---

[5] Backban, Julius, *Pricing: Policies and Practices,* National Industrial Conference Board Inc., New York, 1961, p. 16.

5. *Out-of-Pocket* v. *Book Costs.*
6. *Incremental* v. *Marginal Cost.*
7. *Traceable* v. *Common Costs.*
8. *Direct* v. *Indirect Cost.*
9. *Replacement* v. *Historical Costs.*

Opportunity v. Outlay Costs

Opportunity costs take the form of profits forfeited by using a limited facility for some other purpose. Because cash is usually the scarce resource being used, the firm with more cash than it can utilize can employ outlay costs as a concept. Other firms must learn to calculate the cost of foregone opportunities and include these estimates in such things as capital budgeting problems. Opportunity costs can be estimated by comparing cash outlay costs and possible revenues.

Past v. Future Costs

The concept of past or historical costs v. future is simple to understand. What is most important to learn is there are few if any managerial decisions that should be made on the basis of past costs. Using historical cost for decisions having futurity implies the future will be the same as the past. Future costs rather than past should be calculated for expense control projecting future income statements, capital budgeting, new product decisions, expansion programmes and price-setting.

Short-Run v. Long-Run Costs

Costs that are associated with different levels of production within a system of limited capacity are short-run. When costs are calculated for a system that includes the possibility of expanding capacity, they are considered long-run. The distinction between long- and short-run costs is important when management begins to think of greater sales as an automatic way of spreading overhead. While it may be true that economies of scale are valid in a short-run situation, they may not be true in the long-run.

Variable v. Fixed Costs

Fixed costs are constant within the specified capacity of the system and will not vary with production. Strictly speaking, variable costs are those that vary as a continuous function of production and sales. One must not confuse fixed costs as uncuttable. Break-even analysis is based on distinguishing between fixed and variable costs.

Out-of-Pocket v. Book Costs

Out-of-pocket costs involve current payments to outsiders as opposed to book costs such as depreciation. We mention this concept to point out that in cost analysis, book cost is not the same as the "book cost" referred to by financial analysts. The importance of the concept is obvious in cash flow analysis.

Incremental v. Marginal Cost

Marginal costs are thought of as the additional costs of one more item within a system of fixed capacity. Incremental costs are simply the added costs of going from one level of production to another and they may be long- or short-run. Incremental costs are most important for marketing decisions. Very few decisions will be made on the basis of adding one unit.

Traceable v. Common Costs

Traceable costs can be identified with a particular part or segment of the company. This part may be a product, department or entire plant. Conversely, common costs cannot be identified with one single part of the company but this does not mean they are fixed. The traceability of costs is most important in product mix decisions.

Direct v. Indirect

Accountants distinguish between direct and indirect cost rather than traceable and common. Direct costs are those that can be traced to a particular product.

Replacement v. Historical Costs

Assets are carried on a balance sheet according to their original purchase price (Historical Cost) or the current cost to replace them. For almost any decision, it is the replacement cost that is important. This is basically the same as the distinction between historical and future costs.

Having clarified the distinction between many classes of costs we can see which, if any, have specific bearing on the pricing

TABLE ONE

Output	Price Obtainable	Total Cost	Marginal Cost	Marginal Unit Cost	Total Revenue	Marginal Revenue	Marginal Unit Revenue	Profit
1,000	$6.00	$4,500			$6,000			$1,500
2,000	5.50	7,500	$3,000	$3.00	$11,000	$5,000	$5.00	3,500
3,000	5.00	9,000	2,500	2.50	15,000	4,000	4.00	6,000
4,000	4.00	9,500	1,000	1.00	16,000	1,000	1.00	6,500
5,000	3.00	10,500	1,000	1.00	15,000	—$1,000	—1.00	4,500
6,000	2.00	11,500	1,000	1.00	12,000	—$3,000	—3.00	500
7,000	1.00	13,500	2,000	2.00	7,000	— 5,000	—5.00	—6,500

decision. "The only costs relevant to any decision about price would be the cost to produce and sell added units or the savings in cost from producing and selling fewer units."[6] In addition, it is important that these be future costs rather than historical. Pushing this concept to its fullest, we finally reach the point where we can say that the lowest price one should charge for his product is its marginal cost.

Traditionally, businessmen refuse to sell below average cost but careful analysis shows that in attempting to sell at average cost a firm may actually lose profits.

One concept we have not yet mentioned is sunk costs. These costs are very closely related to fixed costs but differ in one important way. They are not recoverable in any fashion. Their importance to a pricing decision is that they should be ignored.

From the example in Table One, we can see how the economist's model of a price decision could be applied in the actual business experience.

In this example, we see how it is possible to calculate marginal or incremental cost from total cost figures. We can also see the firm maximizes profit by selling at the point where marginal revenue equals marginal cost.

Before leaving the subject of costs and price, let us analyse the businessman's desire to use total costs in making a price decision. In the typical case, a businessman will assume some sales volume. He will calculate his average full cost at that volume then add a percentage profit on to his figure. If the price turns out to have been too high, sales volume does not reach the expected level. The businessman recalculates total cost then gets a new average at the lower volume. Because the volume was lower, the average cost plus margin must lead to a higher price with still lower sales. It is therefore obvious that blind allegiance to full cost plus pricing not only defies the principles but also defies the laws of logic.

Stage of the Life-Cycle

Companies have the greatest freedom of choice when pricing a new product. Few products are really new in that they are the only product available to satisfy a rational economic desire. Within the range delineated by substitute products, the seller of a new product can set a skimming price or a penetration price.

Penetration pricing uses a low initial price to gain a fast and

---

6 Oxenfeldt, op. cit., p. 36.

early foothold in a market. The low initial unit price will also keep unit profits at a low level, thereby inhibiting the inrush of competition. This approach is most suited to those cases when there are close substitute products available.

The opposite of penetration pricing is called skimming pricing. Skimming means setting a high initial price and then reducing the price in successive steps until the theoretical matching of marginal revenue and marginal cost takes place. What the seller is doing in this case is working his way down the demand curve.

Skimming is an acceptable pricing philosophy when a product is unique or has a great deal of patent protection. The philosophy gives management time to learn something about production problems. It also allows the company to test demand at many price levels.

Judgement in Pricing

"There is no way in which the various factors analyzed earlier can be fed into a computing machine to determine the "right" price. Individual factors assume varying importance at different times. Basically it is the judgement of the price maker which is the catalytic agent that fuses these various factors into a final decision concerning price. Pricing is an art, not a science. The "feel" of the market of the price maker is far more significant than his adeptness with a calculating machine. This is why simple formulas for pricing represent a yearning rather than reality. There is widespread recognition of the importance of judgement by academicians and businessmen alike."[7]

We have now covered most of the general pricing problems. Next we will take a look at the specific problem of product-line pricing. After that we will analyse several of the most common pricing techniques now in practice. We will end our discussion of pricing with an analysis of a qualitative and quantitative formula for price setting.

Product Line Pricing

Our reason for discussing product-line pricing is quite simple. The manufacturer of a product line has all the pricing problems of the single-product firm plus a group of unique problems. In addition to the normal problems of pricing new products, determining discount structures and establishing a pricing

[7] Backman, op. cit., p. 60.

philosophy, the manufacturer or seller of a complete line must establish a basic price-line policy and establish the proper relationship between items in the line.

In its broadest interpretation, product-line pricing refers to finding the proper price relationship between members of a product group and also to finding the relationship of different prices charged for the same product under varying conditions. To draw a distinction between these two concepts, we will call differences in price through a product-line product differential; and differences caused by the change of conditions distribution differentials.

Joel Dean lists five possible product-line policies:

"1. Prices that are proportional to full cost, i.e., that produce the same percentage net profit margin for all products.

2. Prices that are proportional to incremental costs, i.e., that produce the same percentage contribution-margin over incremental costs for all products.

3. Prices with profit margins that are proportional to conversion cost, i.e., that take no account of purchased material costs.

4. Prices that produce contribution margins that depend upon the elasticity of demand of different market segments.

5. Prices that are systematically related to that stage of market and competitive development of individual members of the product line."[8]

The first three of Dean's suggested policies are easily shown to be inadequate. They are only related to costs with no mention of demand. It seems that some combination of the fourth and fifth philosophy would be adequate. Perhaps the simplest statement would be that price differentials should be representative of the demand relationships between all members of the product line.

Setting prices that compensate for demand relationships merely recognizes the interrelationship of demand between all products in a line— it also recognizes that there is a time relationship between the sale of products (sales today of A will affect sales of B in ten weeks). This same basic philosophy allows for recognizing the differences in demand elasticity within individual market segments.

Distribution differentials give consideration to the fact that conditions of purchase differ and prices should reflect these differences. There are six general reasons for distribution differentials existing, "(1) Trade status of buyer (functional discounts), (2) Amount of his purchase (quantity discount),

---

8 Dean, op. cit., 473-476.

(3) location of buyer (geographic prices), (4) promptness of payment (cash discounts), (5) time of purchase, and (6) the buyer's personal situation."[9]

Functional Discounts

To compensate for the fact that various types of firms in the marketing channel perform different services, sellers have developed a system of functional discounts. Wholesalers who carry stock may be given a larger discount than a non-stocking wholesaler. Additional discounts may be given to members of the channel who are willing to finance their customers. The seller gives this extra discount in recognition of the fact that he would otherwise have to perform the function.

Quantity Discounts

This type of discount is given with the hope that it will increase profits in one of two ways: Reduce the cost of selling and/or increase the amount sold. If quantity discounts reduce the number of individual transactions without creating production or sales problems, they will usually make marketing more efficient. The seller must balance the savings in costs with the reduction in revenue. Quantity discounts may be used to lower the effective price and thereby take advantage of price elasticity.

Cash Discounts

Money has a time utility. Keeping accounts receivable at a minimum recognizes this utility. The cost of a cash discount must be balanced against the firm's cost of capital. If a firm is willing to give a 2% discount for an immediate cash payment, rather than net in 30 days, they are placing an approximate value of 24% on their capital.

Geographic Discounts

Firms spatially separated from their customers may absorb transportation costs in an effort to minimize the effect of local competition. Elaborate systems of basing point prices have developed to handle the problem of spatial separation.

---

9 Howard, op. cit., p. 376.

Time of Purchase

Sellers of products with seasonal demand patterns might offer discounts during the slow period. These discounts are intended to bring in marginal sales and thereby increase the product's total contribution to margin.

Personal Situation Discounts

Fully negotiated transactions are subject to the varying strength of buyer and seller. Strong buyers may force individual price concessions. These can be thought of as discounts created by personal situations.

Current Methods of Setting Prices

Before looking at how businessmen should set prices, we will quickly review what they are currently doing. Current pricing practices divide into four general categories—Cost plus, Rate of Return, Intuitive and Administered. These four pricing methods are all cost-oriented but the businessman justifies them on three grounds:

"1. Businessmen, as a rule, know much more about product costs than consumer demand.
2. These methods are relatively quick and easy to apply inasmuch as product costs are typically calculated anyway.
3. By and large, these practices are safe."[10]

Cost-plus Pricing

Involves the determination of full allocated costs of production plus a fixed mark-up. It is based on past rather than incremental or marginal costs.

Rate of Return Pricing

Begins with a determination of the physical assets necessary to produce at a specified rate per day. Anticipated usage of all facilities is calculated for a long period of time. (Two or three planning periods). An average investment is then calculated. Average fixed and variable costs are then calculated and added to the average investment. The minimum rate of return acceptable to the company is then added to the total and the result is the suggested price. This method is a slight im-

10 Green, op. cit., p. 24.

110

provement on cost plus but is still based on a cost rather than demand criteria.

Intuitive Pricing

We have previously mentioned the role of judgement in pricing. Intuitive prices are based on executives feeling that they are correct.

Administering Pricing

This concept usually applies to situations where sellers maintain the same selling price over long periods of time. The market is usually oligopolistic with a strong price leader. Non-price competition is more prevalent than price competition.

"Certain common elements appear to stand out which distinguish business practice from economic theory:

1. Businessmen appear to rely on costs much more formally than demand when making pricing decisions. This is in large measure due to their better ability to estimate this side of the coin.

2. The costs chosen, however, are primarily full, historical costs rather than the incremental, future costs of the theoretical economist.

3. The competitive role seems to be taken into account more on a defensive than offensive basis; that is, the implication may be 'leave well enough alone'.

4. Emphasis appears to be more on safeguarding a 'normal profit, than accepting the assumed greater risk associated with the policy of price setting for maximum profit."[11]

Multi-Stage Approach to Pricing[12]

The multi-stage approach to pricing is a six-step procedure. It explains in qualitative terms what the pricing executive must consider when making a pricing decision. The steps are as follows:

1. Select market targets.
2. Select brand image.
3. Select marketing mix.

---

11 Green, op. cit., p. 243.

12 This section is a restatement of material presented by Oxenfeldt in *Pricing for Marketing Executives,* Wadworth Publishing Co., Belmont, California, (c.), reprinted by permission, pp. 63-87, also published by I.B.M. as *Pricing and Forecasting,* pp. B28-55.

4. Select price policy.
5. Select price strategy.
6. Select specific price.

Selection of Market Targets: All marketing decisions including price start with an evaluation of the customers the firm wants to cultivate. Because most firms are precommitted to production facilities and product lines, they do not have complete freedom in their choice of customers. When analysing market segments, the price-setter must also complete a marketing audit, i.e., analysis of his firm's strengths and weaknesses, capabilities, resources, commitments, aspirations, the attitude of management and the capabilities of rival firms.

Selection of Brand Image: When identifying his product with a brand name, a seller hopes to strengthen a brand image. This image must be consistent with the needs of the market segment he is hoping to sell. Brand image is created by product designs, package, channels of distribution, advertising, price and public relations. In a circular type of effect, brand image also determines how you employ each of the above factors. Brand image will determine, in part, how your product's price is perceived.

Selection of a Marketing Mix: In talking about the circular effect of brand image, we have already mentioned selection of the marketing mix. To elaborate slightly, when choosing elements of the marketing mix, the part played by price must be determined. Is the appeal for patronage to be based mainly on price or will other means such as convenience, style, quality, advertising or service be the main appeals?

Selection of a Specific Price Policy: Once the role of price has been determined, management must develop the role into a policy. Policy would answer questions such as "should it establish prices for individual items ... as such ... or as members of a product team; should it rely heavily on special deals; should its prices equal the average of competitors' prices or should they be above or below the average; should it attempt to maintain stable prices or feel free to vary them frequently if there seems to be reason; should it maintain a uniform national price or permit numerous local variations; should it advertise price or should it not; should it make efforts to maintain resale prices or allow sellers to fix prices?" These questions can be answered by choosing the policy that suits the first three areas we discussed.

Selection of a Price Strategy: Market conditions vary from day to day. These daily or longer variations require the pricer to have alternate price strategies to meet new situations. The degree of variation in these strategies is predetermined by the previously made selection of market target, brand image, marketing mix and price policy. These factors leave some room for the development of varying strategies and this freedom of action should be used.

Selection of a Specific Price: From the range of prices available to him, the pricer must finally choose a specific price. If he had full cost and demand information, he could select on the basis of simple arithmetic. Rarely will the pricer have complete information; therefore he must pick specific prices in some other manner. We have already mentioned skimming and penetration strategies. Along with these, a third strategy of maintaining a constant differential with competition can be used to set a specific price.

Oxenfeldt says there are six parties with interest in the pricing decision. We will look at each of these and analyse their effect on the choice of price strategy and specific price.

Other Members of the Firm: Two groups outside of marketing are most vocal in presenting their point of view to the pricer. Finance or the controller's office will usually insist on a product being priced so that it will pay back the initial investment quickly. It is usually someone in the accounting end of the business that insists that every item in a line recoup its full allocated costs. Representatives from manufacturing will usually want initial prices set high enough to cover any unforeseen production problems.

Customers: We have already spent a great deal of time on consumers. There is no need to re-emphasize their importance in the pricing decision.

Potential Rivals: Potential rivals are a most important consideration when introducing a new product. The price strategy of penetration is specifically designed to restrain potential competition. The actions of rival firms must be fully anticipated if a price strategy is to return the highest expected value.

Resellers: When analysing the price final consumers will pay for a product, the price setter must remember the margin he is going to give middlemen. In many cases, the middleman can be your first clue as to what the public will be willing to pay for a product. Understanding the functions played by various

113

types of middlemen will help in deciding price differentials between different classes.

Suppliers: The cost of raw materials, labour and capital are often affected by a company's profitability. These items tend to cost more in a profitable company giving rise to the possibility of higher prices.

Government: Finally, the pricer must always respect the formal and informal power of the government to intercede in almost any price decision.

Information for Pricing

We have mentioned lack of information as one of the reasons sellers do not use demand information in setting prices. We will now take a closer look at the information needs of price setters. The following types of information have direct bearing on most pricing decisions:

(1) price charged by rivals
(2) customers' reactions to prices being charged currently
(3) data on production and distribution costs of the firm and its rivals
(4) relative profitability of items sold by the firm
(5) behaviour of middlemen
(6) cost structure of middlemen
(7) profit of your item with regard to middlemen
(8) position of your item on retailer's shelf
(9) changes in sales by item, area, salesmen,
(10) personality and socio-economic profiles on new customers and lost customers.[13]

All companies would benefit from keeping a market log. The log would have all developments in individual markets that might be pertinent to future marketing decisions recorded in it. Market logs allow reference back into time when new decisions must be made. They rely on immediate impression, rather than recollection of facts, tempered by the passing of time.

There are no simple ways to find out what a customer is willing to pay for a product. It is almost impossible to simulate the market place in experiments and potential customers cannot be expected to be able to predict what they will pay for a product at some later date. There are four basic methods of trying to find out what a customer will pay for a product:

---

13 Oxenfeldt, op. cit., pp. 63 and B-14.

market trial, questionnaire, barter experiments, statistical analysis of past price quantity relationships.

Market Trial: This method calls for introducing a product into several different markets of varying prices. Severe restrictions of expense, time and security prevent market trials from providing fool-proof information. While not a source of precise information, the market trial can prove to be very illuminating.

Questionnaire: Realizing that you cannot ask a customer simply what he will pay, new psychological questioning techniques may prove beneficial to price research. Project techniques seem to have some potential in this area.

Barter Experiments: The barter experiment presents the customer with a real choice under somewhat controlled circumstances. In some cases the person is given money and told to choose one from an assortment of goods. In other cases, the person is given the item to be priced and asked which amongst others he would swap it for. There are limitations on carrying the results of game experiments to the real world, but valuable insights can be gained.

Statistical Analysis: Firms which have been selling in a market for a sufficiently long period of time may have enough past information to run multiple correlation analysis. Few firms have kept enough information to run statistical analysis.

Decision Model for Competitive Bidding

There is one type of pricing problem in which we can overcome some of the problems discussed so far. If a firm has kept a minimum of data, it can utilize a simple probability model for solving the price decision in a competitive bid. In its purest form, competitive bidding calls for each firm to submit a sealed bid; the firm submitting the lowest bid is awarded the contract. How should a firm bid in a competitive bidding situation?

For purposes of this illustration, we will assume the firm has as its objective the maximization of immediate profit. Profit in this case is the difference between the Bid Price and the Expense of completing the project. Symbolically, we might express this as follows: $P = B - E$. We must now return to our concept of expected payoff. The only time the above formulation will represent the true expected payoff on a bid is when there is a 100% probability of getting the reward. If a company knew that its chances of getting a particular contract were 50%, then it could calculate an expected payoff that took this per-

centage into consideration. For example; if "Z" company bids
$10,000 on a project that will cost $9,000 to complete and
it knows the probability of getting the contract is 50%, then
expected profit is as follows:

$10,000 — $9,000 = $1,000
.5 x $1,000 + .5 x 0 = $500

In formula form, the calculation of expected profit is:

$EP = PR (B — E) + (1 — PR)$ x 0

PR = probability of receiving contract.

Using this approach in the business environment requires
knowing the probability of getting a bid at various possible bid
prices. If a company has kept records of its estimated expenses
and the winning bid price on all contracts it has bid on, it can
develop this probability information. It can also calculate the
probability of winning a bid at various prices.

Assume a company to have bid on 100 contracts in the
past. It has kept a record of its estimated expenses to complete
the project if it received the bid. It also has kept a record of all
the winning bid prices.

The probability of winning was calculated as follows:

Winning bid Estimated Expense as a % of cost	Number of times occurring	Prob. of occurrence	Therefore if bid is X% of Est. Exp. Prob. of winning is:	
			Bid	Prob. of Win
.8	1	1%	79%	100%
.9	5	5%	89%	99%
1.0	10	10%	99%	94%
1.1	14	14%	109%	84%
1.2	30	30%	119%	70%
1.3	22	22%	129%	40%
1.4	18	18%	139%	18%
1.5	0	0%	149%	0%
		100%		

There is no history of any bid being less than 80% of the
company's estimated cost, therefore if the company bids 79%
of its estimated cost it is assured of receiving the bid. 1% of
the bids in the past have been between 80% and 90% of the
company's estimated expense of completion; therefore the probability of winning a bid if their bid price is 89% of cost is 99%.
The same type of reasoning follows through for any bid the
company would like to make.

With this information you could then calculate an optimal
bidding strategy. Taking all the possible bids the company

could make, you express the profit or loss that bids would generate in terms of percentage above or below expenses. For example, a bid of 79% of expense would generate a loss of 21%. You then multiply the percentage profit or loss by the probability of its occurence. The result is the expected profit in terms of a percentage over or below expense.

Bid as % of expense	% above or below exp.	Prob. of win	Expected profit in terms of Exp.
79%	—21%	100%	—21%
89%	—11%	99%	—11%
99%	— 1%	94%	— 1%
109%	+19%	84%	+11%
119%	+19%	70%	+13% Optimal Bid
129%	+29%	40%	+12%
139%	+39%	18%	+ 5%
149%	+49%	0%	0%

From this exercise the company knows that in the long run it will maximize profit by bidding 119% of its estimated expenses in all competitive bidding situations.

We see in this example that a price-setter has the tools available to reduce the pricing decision to an arithmetic problem. Even if a firm cannot meet the necessary conditions for automatically accepting the arithmetic answer, it should attempt this type of analysis and then apply outside information to mold the answer to one that fits reality.

The analysis of alternate pricing strategies in the normal selling environment can also be subjected to Bayesian analysis. Through the use of prior and posterior analysis, the price-setter can analyse the effect of different strategies as discounted cash flows. This type of analysis requires the assignment of probabilities to possible competitive reactions. It also requires forecasts of future revenue and costs. The final formulation of a pricing problem in Bayesian terms may have to be a simplification or a generalization of the real world. While a shortcoming of the method, it is not critical. Bayesian analysis will force the decision-maker to understand the pricing environment. It will require an understanding of the implicit generalizations that would have been made in any other type of decision process.

Conclusion

Our purpose in this discussion has been to create an awareness of the full scope of the pricing decision. We have attempted to cover the broad economic, psychological, and corporate problems that must be considered in the pricing decision. While the businessman may not be able to price according to a strict marginal-cost, marginal-revenue formula, he can break away from his older cost-oriented pricing methods. Finally, advances in quantitative analysis make the evaluation of alternate pricing strategies amenable to a rational decision process.

DISCUSSION QUESTIONS

1. How do behavioural science findings relate to the pricing decision?
2. What problems does the businessman face in trying to apply economic models to pricing decisions?
3. What are the relevant costs in any pricing decision?
4. How does the multi-stage approach to pricing bring logic to the pricing decision?
5. Describe how quantitative methods of decision making can be used in the pricing decision.

BIBLIOGRAPHY

ALDERSON & GREEN: *Planning and Problem Solving in Marketing*, Richard D. Irwin Inc., Homewood, Ill., U.S.A.

BACKMAN, JULIUS: *Pricing, Policies and Practices*, National Industrial Conference Board, New York, N.Y., U.S.A., 1961.

DEAN: *Managerial Economics*, Prentice-Hall, Englewood Cliffs, N.J., U.S.A.

HOWARD: *Marketing Management: Analysis and Planning*, Richard D. Irwin Inc., Homewood, Ill., U.S.A.

OXENFELDT: *Pricing and Forecasting*, reproduced by I.B.M., Poughkeepsie, N.Y., U.S.A., 1960.

OXENFELDT, MILLER, SCHUCHMAN, WINICK: *Insights Into Pricing*, Wadsworth Publishing Co., Belmont, California, U.S.A.

SPENCER & SIEGEMAN: *Managerial Economics: Decision Making and Forward Planning*, Richard D. Irwin Inc., Homewood, Ill., U.S.A.

8

Channels of Distribution

THIS discussion of distribution channels will be divided into four parts. First, we will look at the general reasons for a trade channel developing. Second, we will analyse the retailer as part of the trade channel. We will study the various types of retailers that have developed in response to particular trade channel problems. Our third area of focus will be that portion of the trade channel serviced by the wholesale establishment. Finally, we will take a close look at the trade channel as a marketing management problem.

Trade Channel Development

We have already analysed the flow of goods from raw material to consumer in terms of a series of sorts and matches. It would pay to re-emphasize some of the ideas presented by Alderson: "The basic function in marketing is sorting. . . . The term sorting may appear to cover so much territory as to be largely vacuous. Indeed, it resembles the ideas of choosing or deciding in the stream of marketing activity. Sorting is not an empty term because it says something about the way choices are usually made in the market place. The assignment or selection which constitutes the act of sorting is always made with reference to some collection or set of goods. The farmer starts with a mixed lot of produce and sorts out the saleable from the unsaleable items. The central market assembles, or accumulates, goods of like grade and quality for convenience in distribution. The next step of distribution or dispersal to the ultimate market involves allocation of goods. Allocation may be based strictly on the

120

flow of customer orders, but sometimes it is modified or drastically altered by overriding considerations. Finally, there is the characteristic action of the buyer of putting unlike things together to form an assortment."[1]

As with almost every other economic function, part of the sorting function has been taken over by the specialist. Formal economic theory often attributes the creation of form utility to the manufacturer and the creation of space and time utility to what it calls the marketing system. While this division of utility creation may not be as clear cut as the economist presents it, there is adequate proof to show channels of distribution develop as particular firms tend to specialize in the creation of space and time utility.

If an intermediary is to develop between the manufacturer and the retailer, we know from our formulation of a transaction both the potency of the manufacturer's assortment and the retailer's assortment must be increased. We also know that the potency of the assortment held by the intermediary must increase. Some very significant economic advantage must come about by the introduction of an intermediary. This advantage can be described in terms of a theory of minimum transaction. Let us assume a market situation as follows: Product X is manufactured by ten manufacturers. There are two hundred retail outlets selling product X. These retailers are evenly divided between cities A and B. Without an intermediary, it would be necessary for each of the ten manufacturers to call on each of the two-hundred retail outlets, thus creating a total of 2,000 individual transactions. Let us now assume an intermediary establishes itself in cities A and B. These two intermediaries say they will represent each of the ten manufacturers to each of the 100 retail outlets in their cities. The number of transactions is now reduced from 2,000 to 220. The economic advantages of reduced selling and shipping costs far outweigh the increase in cost added by the intermediary.

In today's economy, with the very common separation of centres of production and centres of consumption, the intermediary performs another valuable service. Alderson tells us that the lack of information prevents the clearing of heterogeneous markets. The intermediary acts as an information-processing plant. Manufacturer and retailer both benefit from the sharply reduced costs of gathering and disseminating information.

---

[1] Alderson, *Dynamic Marketing,* op. cit., p. 34.

The final general advantage created by an intermediary is in the reduction of inventory necessary for doing business. Both the retailer and household consumer will carry a smaller inventory because of the speed with which stocks can be replenished by the intermediary. Because the intermediary has intimate knowledge of his market, he requires less stock than a physically separated manufacturer. Finally, the intermediary relieves the manufacturer of the stock-carrying problem.

Channels of distribution are no less dynamic than any other factor in the marketing environment. Each segment of the channel, in its search for differential advantage, introduces a stimulus for change. The number of differing types of intermediaries is almost staggering. We will look at the classical wholesale and retail structures, realizing the firm as it exists in any real market might be very different. Our purpose will be to analyse the problems of each segment in the channel so that we can fully appreciate the problems of a manufacturer who must establish and manage his channels of distribution.

The Retail Channel

Our discussion of retailing will be divided into five parts: (1) the retail product and its consumer, (2) types of retail organizations, (3) small- versus large-scale retailing, (4) general retailing problems and (5) design of retail facilities. Before we can discuss any of the problems of retailing, it will be necessary to define the area. Retailing includes all activities directly related to the sale of goods or services to the ultimate consumer for personal non-business use. A retailer or retail store is a business enterprise which sells primarily to ultimate consumers for non-business use.

Types of Consumer or Retail Products

Retail products are traditionally classified as convenience, shopping and specialty goods. Professor Stanton has developed a chart in which he lists the characteristics and marketing considerations between these three types of products. While not a perfect classification scheme, it serves as a useful framework for generalization.

If one studies Professor Stanton's list of characteristics, one point strikes out very clearly. It is not the product itself, but rather consumer purchasing habits, which determine its classification. Products will shift classification according to who is

122

"CHARACTERISTICS OF CLASSES OF CONSUMER GOODS AND SOME MARKETING CONSIDERATIONS

Characteristics	Convenience	Shopping	Specialty
1. Time and effort devoted by consumer to shopping	Very little	Considerable	Cannot generalize—may go to nearby store ... or go to distant store
2. Time spent planning purchase	Very little	Considerable	Considerable
3. How soon want is satisfied after it arises	Immediately	Relatively long time	Relatively long time
4. Are price and quality compared?	No	Yes	No
5. Price	Low	High	High
6. Frequency of purchase	Usually frequent	Infrequent	Infrequent
7. Importance	Unimportant	Often very important	Cannot generalize

Marketing Considerations:

	Convenience	Shopping	Specialty
1. Length of channel	Long	Short	Short to very short
2. Importance of retailer	Single store ... Unimportant	Important	Very important
3. Number of outlets	As many as possible	Few	Few. Often only one in market
4. Stock turnover	High	Lower	Lower
5. Gross margin	Low	High	High
6. Responsibility for advertising	Manufacturers	Retailers	Joint responsibility
7. Importance of point-of-purchase display	Very important	Less important	Less important
8. Advertising used	Manufacturers	Retailers	Both
9. Brand or store name important	Very brand	Store name	Both
10. Importance of packaging	Very important	Less important	Less important."[2]

---

[2] Stanton, *Fundamentals of Marketing*, McGraw-Hill Book Co., New York, 1964, p. 132.

doing the purchasing. While the possibility of dual classification makes it impossible to identify a single set of purchasing habits for any product, it is no reason for avoiding some type of classification. Each classification serves as a conceptual framework within which the marketing manager must act.

Types of Retailers

The two most common methods of classifying retail outlets are by type of ownership and by the product and service assortment offered. At this point, we will do no more than look at the broad categories; in a later section we will review the problems created by particular retail structures. We should first define two words found in most retailing definitions: variety and assortment. Variety refers to the range of products within a related merchandise line. Assortment refers to the range of choice in a specific product.

General Store: This is a new departmentalized store offering a wide variety of merchandise lines with no natural association and with limited assortments. The general store usually develops in a sparsely settled area and carries a wide variety to maximize total sales potential per individual unit of population. While many modern supermarkets seem to be moving in the general store direction, they are still primarily in the food business.

Limited-Line Stores: A limited-line store offers a wide variety in a single related merchandise line with an extensive assortment. The supermarket is a good example of a limited-line store.

Specialty Store: Limited variety within a single merchandise line with very extensive assortments is offered here. Men's and women's shoe stores would be the typical specialty store. The specialty store should not be confused with the store carrying specialty goods.

Departmentalized Specialty Store: A departmentalized store offers a wide variety within a single merchandise line with extensive assortments. Men's and women's clothing stores would be good examples.

Department Store: Department stores offer a wide variety within related merchandise lines with no natural association, but are so departmentalized that each department resembles a limited-line specialty store.

Full Service: This type of retailing is the traditional case where the customer entered an establishment, was served by a sales person and could then avail himself of a full line of service such as credit, delivery and service.

Limited Service: This is usually a large-scale departmentalized institution offering a wide variety of merchandise operating on a self-service basis and featuring price as the main appeal. Supermarkets are typical limited service stores.

Discount Store Retailing: Modern discount stores are usually large stores, freely open to the public, advertising widely, carrying a fairly wide variety of well-known brands of hard goods, selling below nationally advertised list prices.

Non-Store Retailing: Mail order selling, automatic vending machines, house-to-house selling.

Ownership Patterns: We can make a generalized division between two types of ownership patterns in retailing: independents and chains. The independent is a firm that operates only one establishment in a particular kind of business. A chain operates two or more establishments in the same general kind of business operated by the same firm.

Because of the competitive pressures of the chain, independents have formed groups to regain strength. There are two basic types of groups formed: Retailer Co-operative Chains and Voluntary Chains. In the retail co-operative, several retailers will join into a co-operative effort in the desire to reduce merchandise costs. The organization will often establish its own wholesale subsidiary and buying office. Voluntary chains come about through the efforts of the wholesaler. As co-operatives gain in strength, wholesalers lose business. To regain this business, the wholesaler will negotiate with a group of retailers and promise to provide certain extra services in exchange for the group's patronage. The wholesaler will often provide help in areas such as accounting, in-store promotion, group advertising, store layout, sales training and inventory control.

Problems and Advantages of Size in Retailing

The large centrally managed chain is said to have a great many operating advantages. It is the desire to acquire these advantages that makes the independent join into group activities. We will have a quick look at each of these advantages:
1. Buying power.
2. Buying skill.

3. Low operating costs:
   (a) Integration of wholesale and retail activities.
   (b) Large-scale standardization.
4. Lower prices.
5. Advertising advantage.
6. Ability to experiment.
7. Risk distribution.
8. Ability to demand good location.

The large chain does not gain its advantages at no cost. There are certain disadvantages involved in size.

1. Need for standardization.
2. Limited services.
3. Lack of enterprise differentiation.
4. Personnel problems.

The fact that small-scale retailing still exists and is growing in size says a lot for the advantages in this type of business. The small-scale retailer can take advantage of the following conditions in his fight against the large chain:

1. The explicit costs of doing business are low.
2. May often be a part-time business.
3. Ease of finding a location.
4. Close contact with consumer.
5. Definite store personality.

The small retailer is faced with an almost overwhelming set of inherent disadvantages:

1. Buying handicap.
2. Lack of specialized employees.
3. Advertising disadvantages.
4. Inability to innovate.
5. Capital disadvantages.
6. Lack of managerial ability.[3]

General Problems in Retailing

Whether he be a large-scale retailer, independent or member of a voluntary group, there is a general pattern of retail management problems that the retailer must solve. We will take a brief look at each of the following problem areas:

1. Choosing a store location.
2. Designing store facilities and layout.
3. Providing capital.

---

[3] For a complete discussion of these points see Beckman and Davidson, *Marketing,* Ronald Press, New York, 7th Ed., Chapter 8.

4. Managing merchandise.
5. Selling and promotion.
6. Managing expenses.[4]

Choosing a Store Location

The store location problem can be handled in three phases. First, locating a suitable community, identifying an area within the community that would be suitable and finally, choosing a store site. Davidson and Brown list thirteen factors to be considered in selecting a community:

1. Size of the trading area.
2. Population size, trend and characteristics.
3. Purchasing power.
4. Retail trade potential.
5. Competitive situation.
6. Progressiveness of community.
7. Advertising media available.
8. Credit facilities.
9. Labour market.
10. Delivery systems available.
11. Proximity to supply.
12. Banks and financial institutions.
13. Legal restrictions.[5]

In selecting a location within the community, the retailer can usually choose from five general locations:

1. Central or downtown area.
2. Secondary shopping district or sub-centre.
3. String street location.
4. Neighbourhood location.
5. Isolated location.

Actual site location should depend on an evaluation of the following:

1. Traffic flow.
2. History of site.
3. Other stores.
4. Terms of occupancy.

---

[4] Alexander and Berg, *Dynamic Management in Marketing,* Richard D. Irwin Inc., Homewood, Ill., 1965, ch. 10.

[5] Davidson and Brown, *Retailing Management,* Ronald Press, New York, 2nd Ed., 1960, pp. 50-51.

Designing Store Facilities and Layout

In the short space allotted, it would be impossible to do justice to the subject of planning of retail buildings and facilities. We will simply list a few of the many problems to be encountered:

1. New building *versus* modernizing.
2. Exterior design:
   (a) store front
   (b) marquee
   (c) signs
   (d) entrances
   (e) display windows
3. Interior design:
   (a) flexibility
   (b) flooring
   (c) colour and interim finish
   (d) lighting
   (e) vertical transport
   (f) heating and air conditioning.
4. Fixtures and equipment.

There are several principles that can guide the design or layout of a retail establishment. The objective of any design problem is the optimum use of space. What one is concerned with is the spatial relationships between the various factors necessary to complete the job.

We speak of the layout problem as being one of proximity, size and shape. Proximity deals with the problem of how close various activities must be to each other. Size is simply how much room is needed to complete the activity, and shape deals with the arrangement of the space needed to carry out the activity. "The optimum layout in a retail display seeks to maximize exposure of the goods which are offered for sale."[6] This principle causes a conflict in many cases. Customers often want a retail outlet designed so they can get in and out as quickly as possible. Very often this is not possible when a store has been designed so that the customer is exposed to all items for sale.

Allocation of space in a retail outlet can be based on a combination of the following rules or guidelines:

1. Products that contribute most towards the meeting of corporate objectives should be given the most space.
2. Take advantage of an item's display value.

---

6 Green, *op. cit.*, p. 508.

3. Impulse items should be placed in high traffic areas.
4. Take advantage of the joint demand characteristics of certain products by placing them close together.

Providing Capital

Capitalization problems are no more difficult in retailing than in any other type of business. We deal with the point only because many retailers, especially the small independent, fail to plan their capital requirements.

Retailers, like most businesses, need long-term capital for investment in building and facilities. They also need working capital to meet the operational expenses of the business. New retail outlets must have sufficient capital to carry them into their profitable stage of growth. Capital must be available to finance normal credit and bad debts. There must be a reserve of capital to meet extraordinary events. The small retail merchant is often very unsophisticated in his approach to capitalization problems, but he is by no means unique in his problems.

Managing Merchandise

Merchandise management is concerned with the problems of maintaining the proper goods in stock and then determining how much of these goods to purchase and when to purchase the goods. There seem to be five general sources of information available to the retailer when he has to decide what to purchase:

1. Past records.
2. Suppliers.
3. Customer requests.
4. Marketing research.
5. Competition.

How much and when to purchase are treated very thoroughly in most inventory control manuals. The problems of retail order point and order quantity decisions are very similar to the general businesses' problems in these areas.

Selling and Promotion

Retail managers have the same sales and promotion problems as any other marketing manager. They must find the optimal or at least a satisfactory distribution of funds within the marketing mix.

129

The management of retail selling, again, is no different in its problem areas than personal selling in any other area. Sales personnel must be selected, trained, assigned to a task, supervised, appraised and motivated. Sales promotion problems of retail outlets will be discussed when we cover the general area of promotion.

Managing Expenses

Although we might sound repetitious, the management of expenses in the retail outlet differs very little from the management of any other type of marketing organization's expenses. We will therefore defer discussion of this subject until we deal with control of the marketing effort.

The Wholesale Channel

Our discussion of the wholesale trade channel will cover three general areas. First we will look at the generalized functions of the wholesaler. Second, we will study the various types of wholesalers that have evolved to meet specific trade channel problems. Third, we will look closely at the use of the manufacturer's agent.

What Is Wholesaling?

The orthodox definition of wholesaling would go something like this: "That part of marketing in which goods and services move to various classes of buyers (or agents thereof) who will: (1) engage in the resale of such goods and services with profit in mind; (2) use the goods and services in order to facilitate the production of other goods to be sold with profits in mind; or (3) use the goods and services for various institutional purposes (e.g. educational, charitable, governmental)."[7]

In general, we look at five characteristics to see if a transaction is wholesale: (1) motive of the purchaser, (2) quantity purchased (subject to certain restraints), (3) variety offered for sale, (4) geographic base, (5) price.

Functions of Wholesaling

When looking at the functional aspects of marketing, we often

---

[7] Revzan, *Wholesaling in Marketing Organization*, John Wiley, New York, 1961, p. 2.

divide the marketing job into three broad parts:
1. Exchange:
    (a) Merchandising.
    (b) Buying.
    (c) Selling.
2. Physical distribution:
    (a) Transportation.
    (b) Storage.
3. Facilitating:
    (a) Standardization and grading.
    (b) Financing.
    (c) Communication and research.
    (d) Assumption of risk.

The wholesaling institution is no different from any other marketing institution and must perform each of the above functions. These functions are carried out as a service to manufacturers and buyers.

Merchandising

Planning the composition of a product line and adjusting it to the changing pattern of consumer demand is what we generally mean by the term merchandising. The wholesaler often helps the producer and retailer in this product management function.

For the producer, the wholesaler can be a valuable source of information. Because of his closeness to the retail market and its consumers, the wholesaler can provide the producer with information on consumer demand and buying habits.

The wholesaler can supply the retailer with information valuable to merchandising decisions. Wholesalers can usually educate retail outlets about proposed new products more quickly and with less expense than if the manufacturer tried to do the education. This is especially true in the case of the small manufacturer. Without the wholesaler, it is doubtful if retailers would even know of the products offered for sale by a large segment of the producing community.

Buying

"The wholesaler offers the retailer very important help in the work of buying and assembling his stock. In fact, this constitutes one of his chief justifications for his existence in the economic system."[8] If the typical retailer had to interview the manufacturers' salesmen for each product that he carried, there would be little time left for any other activity. Alderson called the function we are talking about "assorting". The assorting function is the collection of unlike supplies in accordance with some pattern determined by demands in order to develop complementarity and to possess some degree of potency for meeting future contingencies. We often refer to the wholesaler as the retailer's purchasing agent.

Selling

In many cases manufacturers regard wholesalers as a natural extension of their own sales force. While this may be the ideal case, it is also a source of conflict in the channel structure. For a wholesaler to be truly marketing oriented, he must be most concerned with the needs of his consumers and not the needs of his supplier.

The wholesaler's existence is often justified on the basis of his providing a sales force for many small manufacturers who could not otherwise reach the market. Certain types of wholesalers do become a producer's only sales force when they purchase his entire production.

Retailers' sales personnel may get their only sales training from a wholesaler. The wholesaler is often a much more able sales trainer than the manufacturer. His intimate knowledge of local conditions is a prime factor in his ability to do this training.

Transportation

An entire class of middlemen has developed to handle the complexities of transportation problems. Organizations, such as freight forwarding agents, exist for the sole purpose of providing transportation service. The wholesaler or middleman developing a specialization in transportation is taking advantage of the dynamic nature of marketing. This dynamic nature provides opportunity to any form of organization that creates some type of utility. Wholesalers specializing in transportation service create utility by reducing the cost of transportation and providing a saving to his customer.

---

[8] Alexander and Berg, *Dynamic Management in Marketing,* Richard D. Irwin Inc., Homewood, Ill., 1965, p. 222.

Storage or Carrying Inventory

A basic responsibility of a marketing system is to have merchandise available that consumers want and to have it available where and when they want it and in the amount they desire. Because we want a marketing system to provide for a rapid flow of goods to the consumer, the burden of carrying inventory would normally fall on the retailer. Wholesalers have come into existence to specialize in this storage function and thereby reduce the retailers' inventory costs.

Standardization and Grading

Agricultural and raw materials marketing is plagued with the problems of standardization and grading. The primary purpose of most local wholesale markets in farm areas is to collect, grade and standardize the heterogeneous assortment of goods delivered by the farmer. Standardization and grading is an essential factor in the selling of "Nature's" produce. Both producer and purchaser reap economic rewards from the wholesaler performing this service.

Financing

Wholesalers provide financing for both the retailer and the manufacturer. The retailer receives two types of credit advantages in purchasing from the wholesaler. First, there is the normal extension of trade credit. Second, and of equal importance, the wholesaler reduces the retailer's need for large amounts of credit by reducing the retailer's need for large inventories.

The manufacturer benefits from wholesale credit in several ways. He can usually discount his wholesaler's accounts payable easier than he could discount a retailer's notes. By placing his produce in a bonded warehouse, the manufacturer can often borrow money against the warehouse receipt. Finally, it is just easier to control the allocation of credit to a small number of wholesalers than controlling the same dollar value of credit to many retailers.

Communication and Research

It is not unusual to find a wholesaler placing advertising that is of direct benefit to both manufacturer and retailer. It is also a common occurrence to find the large wholesaler a vital link in the marketing research process.

Risk Assumption

Finally, we come to one of the most important functions performed by the wholesaler. The wholesaler relieves the manufacturer and the retailer of much of the risk involved in carrying inventory. As products move from manufacturer to consumer, a very large part of the risk burden is placed on the channel of distribution. In those channels where storage is an important factor, this assumption of risk is of utmost importance.

Types of Wholesale Institutions

It would be impossible to critically evaluate the many types of wholesale institutions that exist in a book of this nature. At best we can list and define the major institutions. Wholesalers can be divided into two general categories: merchants and agents. Merchants as a rule purchase the product, take possession and title. Agents very often act only as a negotiating intermediary and seldom take title or possession of the goods being sold.

Merchant Type Wholesalers

Regular or Service Wholesaler: This type of wholesaler is the largest and most significant institution in the wholesaling field. He purchases and carries an inventory and provides the full range of services we have discussed. This group is often divided into three further categories: general merchandise wholesalers, who carry a wide variety of merchandise in a number of unrelated lines; general line wholesalers, who carry a wide variety of merchandise in a single merchandise line; specialty wholesalers, who specialize in a few items in a single line.

Industrial Distributor: This wholesaler, who is sometimes called the mill supply house, varies from the regular wholesaler in two ways. He specializes in buying and selling of industrial goods. Secondly, he tends to locate only in areas of heavy industrial concentration.

Importers-Exporters: These wholesalers deviate from the regular wholesaler in that they purchase only from foreign-based sources and/or sell to foreign-based buyers.

Cash-and-Carry Wholesaler: All sales are on a cash basis and deliveries are made only at a fee. Items carried are usually restricted to those having a high rate of turnover. Cash-and-carry wholesalers sometimes exist as departments within the regular or full service wholesaler.

Drop Shippers or Desk Jobbers: In this type of organization, delivery of the product goes from producer to consumer. Billing goes producer, wholesaler, consumer. It is most prevalent in those industries where transport costs are high, relevant to total product value.

Mail Order Wholesaler: As the name implies, this type of wholesaler depends on a mail order catalogue to generate sales.

Truck Waggon Jobbers: This type of middleman carries his produce on a truck or waggon and makes regularly scheduled visits to his customers. Deliveries are made directly from the stock he is carrying on his vehicle.

Manufacturers' Sales Branches: These are owned by manufacturers and mining companies and maintained apart from the manufacturing plant for the purpose of marketing their products at wholesale.

Converter: Existing primarily in the textile industry, the converter purchases grey goods from small textile manufacturers and then does the dyeing and cutting of the cloth. The converter sells to the manufacturers who produce textile products.

Wholesaler-Sponsored Voluntary Chains and *Retail-Sponsored Voluntary Chains:* These two groups were covered in our discussion of retailing.

Agent Type Wholesalers

Auction Company: Primarily in the livestock and primary produce industries, this type of wholesaler takes physical possession, arranges for display, prepares catalogues, conducts auctions and arranges for collection of the sales proceeds.

Commission Agents: Usually found in the produce area, this wholesaler performs all of the functions of the regular wholesaler except for taking ownership.

Export-Import Agents: These middlemen are the agent counterparts of the exporter and importer who take title and possession of goods.

135

Brokers: Representing buyers and sellers, but not both parties, the broker either negotiates for or brings the parties together for negotiation. They often act to find a purchaser for the entire output of a small manufacturer. The broker will sometimes have authority to choose a final set of terms of sale but usually they must be approved by the party he is representing.

Selling Agents: When a manufacturer is too small to afford his own sales force, he will hire a sales agent to represent him. The sales agent usually has the authority to negotiate price. He will often provide financial assistance to the manufacturer. The pure form of sales agent is not assigned to any particular territory.

Manufacturers' Agents

"The manufacturers' agent is an independent business establishment that sells on a continuous contractual basis in a limited or exclusive territory, a part of the output of two or more client manufacturers whose products are related but non-competing. The agent does not take title to the goods in which he deals but he is paid a commission and has little or no control over prices, credit or terms of sale."[9]

The manufacturers' agent possesses some distinct advantages for the company using him: (1) Sales costs are not incurred until an actual sale takes place. Personal selling expenses as a percentage of sales are fixed. (2) When properly used, the agent will be a more economical sales force than a company's own sales force. (3) Ability to provide intensive geographic coverage. (4) Close knowledge of market. (5) Eliminates many problems of sales administration. (6) Agents often of high calibre and broad experience. (7) Immediate entry into the market possible.

Advantages don't come without disadvantages: (1) The agent may eventually become more costly than your own sales force. (2) Little ability to control agent's sales force. (3) Only getting part of agent's time. (4) Chance of losing a complete market if agent drops manufacturer. (5) Little chance to meet final customers.[10]

---

[9] Staut and Taylor, *A Managerial Introduction to Marketing,* Prentice-Hall, N.J., 1965, p. 273.

[10] See Staut and Taylor, op. cit., for more complete discussion—chapter 15.

Channel Management

Channels of distribution can be managed. A product's channel of distribution is not pre-ordained. It is possible to mould and shape the channel a product follows in the same way you control internal corporate structure. Many of the principles that are relevant in developing corporate structure are appropriate in designing trade channels.

Our discussion will cover the following points: (1) Nature of the distribution problem; (2) Factors affecting the channel decision; (3) Developing channel alternatives; (4) Evaluating the alternatives; (5) Administration of the channel; (6) Quantitative methods in channel management.

Nature of the Distribution Problem

Distribution problems can be handled within the same general framework as all other marketing problems. Trade channel management is concerned with the development of the optimal combination of institutions through which a product moves on its way to consumers.

Solution of the distribution problem starts with much the same information as the solution of any problems in the marketing mix area! Identify the product's ultimate consumer and structure the marketing organization to meet this consumer's needs. When the following questions can be answered about a product's customers, one half of the trade-channel problem is solved.

1. Who is the consumer?
2. What does he purchase?
3. Where does he purchase?
4. When does he purchase?
5. How does he purchase?
6. What else in the company's current or future product line would the consumer like to purchase?
7. Where would the consumer like to purchase?
8. When would the consumer like to purchase?
9. How would the consumer like to purchase?

The second part of the trade-channel problem is solved when the following questions are answered:

1. What current or potential trade channels are available?
2. What trade channels will best satisfy the company's marketing objectives?

137

Perhaps the hardest part of establishing or changing a trade channel is realizing that the channel is not fixed. The trade channel can and should be used as a competitive tool in the same way as price, advertising, packaging and service. Enterprise differentiation is particularly important to industries that react in a self-destructive manner in the face of price competition.

Presenting a product to the market through a unique trade channel can be a powerful competitive advantage. Each member firm in an industry may think it sells to the same group of final customers. In reality, customers are a heterogeneous mass, each with specific needs. The trade channel that does most to satisfy these needs will not be the same for all customers. It follows that your trade channel may not be optimally designed if it attempts to satisfy all possible customers. In fact, such a trade channel may prevent the satisfaction of any group of customers.

Factors Affecting Channel Decision

For purposes of this discussion, we will assume that the company under question has conducted a market survey and has identified its customers, knows their purchasing habits and understands their needs. It will also be assumed that the company has clearly defined its objectives.

The person responsible for developing a channel strategy should start his job with a distribution audit. Product, customers and inherent corporate abilities and the external environment should be analysed for their influence on the channel decision.

Analysing the product will identify its needs in the area of finance, handling, storage and selling effort required. To identify specific requirements in the above areas, the analyst must review the following product characteristics: unit value, bulk and weight, technical nature, perishability, fashion, seasonality, standardization, stage of market development, length of line. We will look at each of these factors very quickly.

Unit Value: Products with high unit value have a tendency towards direct channels. High value does not demand direct channels but low value seems to require the use of wholesalers. Unit value will be a determinant of the amount of risk associated with individual sales.

Bulk and Weight: If bulk and weight are such that carload

138

shipping is necessary, the need for a wholesaler to reduce shipping costs is reduced. Weight-to-value factors will determine the geographic distribution pattern. If the end product is bulkier than the raw material, manufacturers will tend to be small and local in nature, often not requiring the use of wholesalers.

Technical Nature of the Product: Highly technical products usually are sold direct. Technical products raise the need for trained service specialists before and after sale. In consumer industries where direct selling may be impossible, the service requirement often causes service centres to be established to maintain consumer good will.

Perishability: If a product is perishable, the manufacturer will want a channel that moves the product quickly and one that can make provisions to prevent deterioration. These conditions often lead to the use of agents who do not take possession, or direct selling. In products which are technologically perishable, the market place has developed leasing as a means of preventing severe loss to the consumer. In general, the more perishable the product the shorter the channel.

Fashion: Highly fashioned goods suffer from a particular type of perishability. With highly fashion-sensitive products, the risks of inventory loss are large and cannot easily be pushed onto channel members. Fashion goods are most always sold direct. In many parts of the fashion goods industry, it is the retailer who seeks out the manufacturer.

Seasonality: Seasonality can occur on both the production and consumption side of a product's life. Products with seasonal consumption patterns cause more channel problems than products with seasonal production. Middlemen will not want to assume out-of-season storage, requiring the manufacturer to carry out the function. This often induces the manufacturer to integrate vertically.

Standardization: "When a product is standardized in the sense (a) that all units of it, regardless of who makes them, are of a substantially uniform characteristic and quality, or (b) that all units sold under one brand are identical or practically so, there is no compelling need for direct contact between the maker and the user every time a sale is made. Such a product can be marketed through indirect channels, with several intermediaries."[11]

---

[11] Alexander, op. cit., p. 280.

Stage of Market Development: For new products without wide acceptance and requiring aggressive promotion, the normal indirect channel is usually ineffective. In this case the manufacturer will resort to exclusive distribution, direct selling or indirect channels backed up by a direct sales force.

"As a product becomes known and gains wide market acceptance and preference, its maker may find that his interests are best served by more general distribution by a larger number and variety of outlets which function more as conduits rather than pumps. At this stage he is apt to rely heavily on advertising to pull his merchandise through these relatively undynamic channels."[12]

Length and Breadth of Line: Manufacturers of long lines and many products sold in the same market will tend towards direct channels. Great care must be exercised before a company decides to use a single direct sales force in vastly different markets.

In order to prevent any possible misunderstanding, it is necessary to repeat several facts. The nature of the product is only one of several parts of the distribution problem. A problem of equal importance is the nature of the customer and how he is going to use the product. The channel manager must have complete socio-economic data about his customers. He must know how many customers there are, how frequently they purchase and what use they are going to make of the product. Each of these factors will have as strong an influence on the channel decision as the nature of the product.

Company Characteristics: Specific aspects of the company situation will play an important part in the channel decision. Three of the most important seem to be; financial strength, reputation, market standing and objectives.

Financial Strength: Developing a marketing channel from scratch can be very expensive. Companies with limited resources can rarely afford to develop either unique or direct marketing channels. A well-financed company can afford the expense of setting up the ideal channel. In the long run, the ideal channel is the cheapest to establish and maintain.

Reputation: New and unknown companies cannot afford the luxury of being overly choosy when deciding on who will represent them. The strong, well-known company can pick and choose his representative from the best available. The com-

---

12 Ibid., p. 280.

pany with a well-established product can almost force firms to carry his product because of customer demand.

Objectives and Policies of the Manufacturer: Channels of distribution must be able to help the manufacturer reach his objectives. Companies selling the same product with different objectives will select different channels. The manufacturer's policy towards price, advertising, service and sales must be considered in the channel decision.

Competition and the External Environment: "The manager who is trying to break into a market should view with respect the channels used by the firms already in it. This does not mean that they should slavishly follow their example, but it does mean he should have good reason for not doing so."[13]

Finally the external environment will cause many restrictions on a management's ability to choose its channel. We have already mentioned competition. Other considerations are general distribution structure in the industry unions, suppliers, government restrictions, and general economic conditions.

Developing Trade Channel Alternatives

Having completed the distribution audit, the channel analyst now possesses the necessary tools to design a channel of distribution. With the preliminary statement of marketing objectives as his guideline, the channel analyst must develop alternative channels for evaluation. The analyst will have to review the job to be done and locate existing, or develop new channels that can do the job.

It will be important for the analyst to remember his organization theory. First, the work to be done is analysed and described. Then the organization is built to do the job. History shows that a great many companies ignore this sequence. These companies design the trade channel according to some preconceived idea and then assign work to each section of the channel.

Building the actual channel should start with a detailed segmentation of the product's end users. This will guarantee that each customer's unique requirements will be considered. Working backwards, the analyst picks groups of middlemen that can best satisfy the groups below them. What actually happens in this process is as follows. A series of heterogeneous customer

---

13 Ibid, 284.

groups is identified, next a smaller group of less heterogeneous middlemen who can effectively cover the customer groups is picked. The process continues until the company is satisfied it can work with the last group of middlemen chosen. The process may end at any stage. The channel that evolves should be an optimal match of corporate ability and customer needs.

Some artificial device is usually necessary to insure that all possible alternative channels are examined. Managements have a tendency to skip over any alternative route that is not currently being used by some company. Any device used for generating alternatives will produce many useless suggestions. Some alternatives can be discarded immediately, others should be examined for possible adoption.

Evaluating and Selecting the Channel of Distribution: How can the channel analyst choose one or two channel programmes out of the many possibilities produced in the generation of alternatives? If he has done his job properly, the analyst at some time made up a list of all factors affecting the channel decision. Working with this list, each alternative channel programme could be evaluated for its interaction with the controlling factor.

As an example, let us assume a product "X". We will also assume that only four factors have any bearing on the channel decision. The analyst in this case has developed three possible channels for the product. He has set up the following matrix showing the factor, the alternative and the demands of the alternative for the factor.

	Alternative A	Alternative B	Alternative C
Warehouse space	100,00 sq. ft.	10,000	50,000
Number of salesmen	5	15	20
Competitive reaction	Low	High	High
Advertising budget	$50,000	$10,000	$20,000

The relationship of each alternative to the controlling factor could then be compared to a list of corporate abilities or policies. In the above example, assume the company had 200,000 sq. ft. of idle warehouse space, very few salesmen with poor prospects of hiring more and a strong capital position, but they had suffered losses to strong competitive reactions. It would be obvious to choose alternative "A". The decision will never be that simple, but this type of decision matrix can be most useful.

The above example did not mention profitability of alternative channels. It is the author's feeling that profitability tests should not be instituted until the list of alternatives has been screened and reduced to size. Quantitative analysis will allow the decision-maker to choose the course of action which will most probably meet the company's profit objective. Each alternative should be evaluated in terms of payoff. The problem reduces to one of decision-making under risk.

Selecting the Specific Middleman

Once the manufacturer decides on a channel, he must select the specific outlets within the channel. If he wants general, broad coverage, he may take any or all firms that pass credit evaluation. His only considerations are cost of sales, order handling and delivery.

In the more selective situation, there are nine factors the channel manager can look at to choose specific outlets: promise of continuity, trading area, trade standing and reputation, other products handled, selling personnel and methods, outlets objectives, stock carrying performance, financial position and facilities.[14]

Continuity: When marketing through someone else's organization, there is always a chance that they will be out of business or drop your product at a very inconvenient time. In general, it is wise to avoid the less permanent types of business organizations.

Trading Area: When selecting particular outlets, the channel manager will try to match outlets with trading areas so that all centres of demand will be covered.

Trade Standing: A merchant's reputation amongst customers and competition is an important factor to consider in selecting an outlet. Certain outlets will lend their prestige to your product or vice versa.

Other Products Handled: In addition to choosing an outlet whose products will aid the sale of his product, the channel manager will want to choose an outlet handling products of equal quality.

Sales Personnel and Methods: The channel manager will want to ensure that an outlet's sales personnel and methods are consistent with his product's needs.

Outlet Objectives: The outlets chosen must have objectives

Marketing, Ronald Press, New York, 7th Ed.
14 Ibid., pp. 294-298.

which aid the sale of your product. Some outlets will want a product simply to prevent competition from getting it.

Stock Carrying Performance: If you want an outlet to carry stock, it is wise to check their past history in this area.

Financial Position: Any outlet chosen should have the necessary financial strength to carry out a proper marketing programme.

Facilities: Simply stated, an outlet must have proper facilities to meet the service needs of the product being sold.

Administration of the Channel

If a company realizes that it can manage its channel of distribution, there should be no real problems of administration. A natural outgrowth of realizing a channel can be managed is the appointment of a channel manager. This man's responsibility would be the day-to-day maintenance of the channel. He would administer and be responsible for the analysis of trade channel contracts, pricing structure, sales training, advertising, inventory control, accounting and other problems of mutual interest to manufacturer and wholesaler.

If the trade channel is to be used as a competitive tool, it should be administered as such. Few firms would run advertising or sales campaigns without the appropriate management. Yet many firms have failed to realize the need for someone to manage the channel of distribution.

Quantitative Methods in Channel Management

We can do no more in this section than mention the general quantitative methods that are applicable to the problems of channel management.

The most powerful decision-making tool available when the initial channel is being selected is Bayesian analysis. By forcing himself to analyse the relevant alternatives, all possible competitive reactions and all possible payoffs, the channel analyst should make the best possible choice. To structure the channel decision in terms of Bayesian analysis, the decision-maker would take the following steps. First he would identify all possible channel alternatives available. He would then try to identify all possible competitive reactions to each different alternative. Next, the analyst would assign probability estimates to each possible competitive reaction. Finally he would calculate the expected value of each alternative.

The manufacturer with several different manufacturing plants scattered around the country usually has a problem of what products to ship to which warehouses or wholesalers. The problem arises because each plant does not have the capacity to supply the full needs of the warehouse it can ship to most cheaply. By use of a simple algorithm, it is possible to calculate lowest total cost arrangement for shipping.

The above problem assumes plant capacity is equal to warehouse requirements. In many cases this is not the situation. In fact, it is often necessary to allocate production to those outlets which provide maximum profit. Deciding who should and should not receive the plant output is connected with the problems of channel management. Combined methods of linear programming and Bayesian analysis can lead to the solution of this type of problem.

Managements are often called on by members of their channel of distribution for help in problems of store layout. Associated with the store layout problem is the concurrent problem of balancing the desire for quick service on the part of the customer and the desire for minimum staff by the outlet's management. Solution to this type of problem can be found within the framework of queuing theory. The problem of how many servicemen to hire, how many trucks to purchase, also falls within the scope of queueing theory.

Most of the pure logistical problems of channel management are amenable to solution through various quantitative methods.

Conclusions

We have moved a long way in our discussion of trade channels. Our primary purpose was to show that the trade channel can be managed and that the position of trade channel manager is not completely unrealistic. When one does finally realize that channels of distribution are a competitive tool and not simply a necessary evil, then we can expect some radical departures from the classical distribution structures.

Marketing: the Management Way

DISCUSSION QUESTIONS

1. Why do trade channels develop?
2. Is the small retailer on the way out?
3. How does the wholesaler serve the manufacturer and retailer?
4. What factors should be considered in a channel-building decision?
5. Describe the management approach to channel building.

BIBLIOGRAPHY

ALDERSON: *Dynamic Marketing Behaviour*, Richard D. Irwin Inc., Homewood, Ill., U.S.A.

ALEXANDER & BERG: *Dynamic Management in Marketing*, Richard D. Irwin Inc., Homewood, Ill., U.S.A.

BARTELS, ROBERT: *Comparative Marketing: Wholesaling in Fifteen Countries*, Richard D. Irwin Inc., Homewood, Ill., U.S.A.

BECKMAN & DAVIDSON: *Marketing*, Ronald Press, New York, N.Y., U.S.A.

CLEWETT (Ed.): *Marketing Channels for Manufactured Products*, Richard D. Irwin Inc., Homewood, Ill., U.S.A.

DAVIDSON & BROWN: *Retailing Management*, Ronald Press, New York, N.Y., U.S.A.

MILLER & STARR: *Executive Decisions and Operations Research*, Prentice-Hall, Englewood Cliffs, N.J., U.S.A.

REVZAN: *Wholesaling in Marketing Organization*, Wiley, New York, N.Y., U.S.A.

STANTON: *Fundamentals of Marketing*, McGraw-Hill, New York, N.Y., U.S.A.

STAUDT & TAYLOR: *A Managerial Introduction to Marketing*, Prentice-Hall, Englewood Cliffs, N.J., U.S.A.

9

Advertising Management

CRITICS of advertising management often make the following charge: "If I spent as much money with as little proof of its value, I would be thrown out on my ear." Perhaps the critics are correct. Our study of advertising management will look at the reasons why the charge arises and why it has been difficult to refute its implications.

Before starting an analysis of advertising specifically, we will take a quick look at the general field of promotion. An attempt will be made to outline the criteria for deciding between the various major forms of promotion. Our discussion will then lead into an analysis of advertising planning. The planning discussion will deal with appraising the advertising opportunity, determining advertising objectives, and establishing the advertising appropriation.

The physical evidence of advertising becomes "copy" in a particular "media". Development of copy and media strategy will be covered in a later part of our discussion.

We began this introduction with a statement about evaluating advertising effectiveness. After using his copy and media strategy, the advertising manager must attempt to evaluate his performance. This is a difficult and complex job. We will only be able to scratch the surface of the area in our discussion.

The final section of our discussion will deal with the client-advertising agency relationship. It is often the relationship between these two parties that determines the success or failure of a particular campaign.

What Is Promotion?

Marketing as a language is filled with its own peculiar jargon. One particular area where confusion seems to abound is in the differentiation of the various forms of promotion. The American Marketing Association defines selling as: "The personal or impersonal process of assisting and/or persuading a prospective customer to buy a commodity or a service or to act favourably upon an idea that has commercial significance to the seller."[1] For our purposes, the words selling and promotion are synonymous. We favour the use of promotion as there is a connotation in the word selling that a transfer of title has taken place. Within the broad definition of promotion, we find subheadings of advertising, personal selling, sales promotion, publicity and some other selling tools such as packaging.

Let us now take a look at each type of promotion and develop working definitions. These are by no means the only possible meanings attached to advertising, personal selling, sales promotion and publicity. They are presented simply as a background for a uniform understanding of this discussion.

Advertising: A non-personal presentation that has as its purpose the promotion of ideas, goods or services by an identified sponsor. The message is paid for and is usually disseminated through one or more of the mass communications media.

Personal Selling: The process of personally assisting and persuading a prospect to buy a commodity or a service or to act upon an idea.

Sales Promotion: "Those selling activities that supplement both advertising and personal selling, co-ordinate them, and render them more effective. It includes sampling, displays, demonstrations, and various kinds of non-recurrent selling effort."[2]

Publicity: "Any form of commercially significant news items or editorial comment about products or institutions published in space or broadcast time that is not paid for by the sponsor."[3]

Conditions for Effective Advertising

Deciding on the basic mixture of personal and non-personal promotional tools is a complex problem which is better left until

---

1 Committee on Definitions, R. Alexander, Chairman, A.M.A. *Marketing Definition—A Glossary of Marketing Terms,* A.M.A., Chicago, 1960, p. 21.
2 Op. cit., Beckman, p. 416.
3 Ibid., p. 416.

the later part of our discussion. At this point we will discuss the general conditions that should exist to make advertising most effective. Professor Neil Borden, in his book, *The Economic Effects of Advertising,* lists certain conditions that govern advertising opportunity. While these criteria are not universal in their application, they do provide a worthwhile framework for thinking about your advertising opportunity.

Borden introduces five conditions which tend to make the use of advertising effective:

"1. Advertising is likely to be more effective if a company is operating with a favourable primary demand than if it is operating with an adverse trend.

2. The second condition governing a concern's opportunity to influence its demand is the presence of large chances for product differentiation.

3. A third condition bearing upon the advertising opportunity for any product is the relative importance to the consumer of hidden qualities of the product as contrasted with external qualities which can be seen and appreciated.

4. A fourth condition having a highly important bearing upon the opportunity for use of advertising to increase the demands of individual concerns is the presence of powerful emotional buying motives which can be employed in advertising appeals to consumers.

5. A fifth condition of importance in determining the employment of advertising to increase the demand of the individual concern is whether the concern's operations provide substantial sums with which to advertise and promote its products in markets it seeks to reach."[4]

With these postulates set out, let us look at why they are true. An expanding demand or growing trend provides a form of inertia in which it is possible to garner the benefits of advertising. There are many examples where companies have lost market share in an expanding market because of a failure to keep up the pace of advertising. We are interested in the use of advertising in an expanding market because it can be used to shift a demand curve. By this we mean that the advertising will increase the effective demand at each price level rather than at only one level.

The ability to differentiate your product from all others makes the advertising job easier and more effective. If a market segment has been identified as having specific needs and a product can be differentiated so that it obviously meets these needs, it stands to reason that advertising has a good chance to be effec-

---

4 Borden, Neil H., *The Economic Effects of Advertising,* Richard D. Irwin Inc., Homewood, Illinois, 1944, pp. 424-425.

149

tive. The degree to which a product can be differentiated will generally govern the profit margin; this will often determine what is to be spent on advertising. This leads us into the fifth postulate or governing factor. Advertising, to be effective, is quite often an expensive proposition. Where little physical differentiation between competing products exists, the competing forces of low profit margin and the need for large advertising budgets are often in conflict. If we look very closely at those products where advertising is the major means of creating product differentiation, we find promotional expenses at a disproportionately high level.

From the viewpoint of advertising effectiveness, product differentiation should not be in a form that is immediately visible. If the purchaser can easily check the validity of an advertising claim of difference, the advertising effect is quickly tempered by the customer's visual or physical check. What we are saying at this point is, with products such as fashion goods and fresh vegetables, the customer can quickly check the physical quality. In an automobile or piece of machinery, the important mechanical features are incomprehensible to the consumer and the advertisement has more chance to have its validity accepted without investigation.

Finally, experience has shown us that those products which can call upon an emotional appeal are good candidates for effective advertising.

It must be stressed at this point that the opportunity to advertise does not depend on these five factors always being present. It depends more on the way these factors are combined in the real world. If one thinks about each of the conditions we have stated, he can usually cite an example of where the factors were in the reverse condition and advertising was still effective. The combination of three positive conditions may simply outweigh the negative factors. Our purpose in presenting these factors is to provide a frame of reference rather than to have them act as decision tools.

It is important to emphasize at this time that Professor Borden is primarily interested in the problem of advertising as an effective tool in the stimulation of selective demand. Some value could be gained at this time in quickly reviewing the conditions that allow for the stimulation of primary demand.

Professor Frey, in his book *Advertising*, suggests that there are seven factors affecting advertising's ability to stimulate primary demand: (1) identity of present users and non-users, (2) wants satisfied by the product, (3) competing wants, (4) nature and strength of available product appeals, (5) alternative ways of satisfying the wants, (6) nature and strength of appeals available for alternative products, (7) social and environmental trends affecting demand.[5]

Before hoping to expand primary demand, an advertiser must be able to identify both the product group's users and non-users. He must be able to identify the non-users so that he can isolate the reasons for non-use.

There is strong evidence to show that advertising can be used to increase primary demand on products that satisfy strong basic consumer needs. Products satisfying the more secondary needs are more effectively promoted on a selective basis. Very closely tied into the type of wants being satisfied as a determinant of advertising's ability to stimulate primary demand is the nature of competing wants. If, in the hierarchy of consumer wants, your product has been displaced by a product meeting a more basic need, the opportunity to expand primary demand is limited. Another closely allied principle in this area works in both primary and selective demand expansion. Products whose appeals satisfy strong emotional needs are good candidates for advertising.

Two factors associated with competing products govern the effectiveness of primary demand stimulation. If a large number of ready substitutes are available, it may pay to concentrate on selective-demand stimulation. If this same multitude of products appeals to strong basic or emotional needs, the effectiveness of primary-demand stimulation through advertising seems to be limited.

Finally, it is not reasonable to expect advertising to have the strength to stop the basic flow of social and environmental change. Strong adverse trends caused by a basic change in the environment are not good candidates for advertising expenditure.

We see that there is a good deal of similarity between the factors affecting the stimulation of primary and secondary demand. But there are enough differences to warn the businessman when he is making an obviously bad choice in advertising objectives.

The Promotional Mix

If one reduces the promotional mix problem down to its basic core, you find four general factors have primary influence on

---

[5] Frey, *Advertising,* 3rd Ed., Ronald Press, New York, 1961.

the balance between personal and non-personal promotion: (1) the amount of money available for promotion, (2) the nature of the market, (3) the nature of the product, (4) stage of life cycle.

We have already mentioned that effective advertising usually requires large sums of money. The weaker and less financially capable a company, the more its leaning should go towards a personal selling approach. While the per capita cost of contact may be much higher when using personal salesmen as opposed to mass advertising, it may be the only alternative available to those companies that cannot afford the cost of effective advertising.

When talking of the nature of the market, we are referring to such things as geographic area covered, the degree of concentration and type of customer. In general, we can say the smaller the geographic spread within the market, the greater the reliance on personal selling. Concentration of market affects the promotional mix in several ways. First, the fewer the number of customers, the easier to cover with personal selling. The greater the diversity of customer types and product usage, the tendency towards impersonal promotion grows. We can make very few generalizations about the relationship of customer type and promotional mix. In general, promotional campaigns directed towards industrial users and middlemen will be more intensive in their use of personal selling than similar campaigns directed at household consumers.

One cannot make the generalization that consumer goods require one type of promotion while industrial goods require another. Within the broad category of consumer goods, we go to both extremes. "Convenience Goods" are most often very intensive in their use of impersonal promotion. "Speciality Goods," on the other hand, may depend entirely on personal selling. Much the same holds true in the industrial field. Raw materials are rarely advertised; yet other industrial products are advertised very heavily. Our conclusion then is that the nature of the product is important, but we cannot make any sweeping generalizations relating the nature of a product to the type of promotion needed.

Within the framework of product life cycle, there are certain generalizations that can be made about promotional strategy. During the introduction stage, personal selling and very limited use of impersonal promotion seems to be most effective. During the growth stage and the period of expanding demand, it seems that advertising is most effective. It is during the period of maturity that a company must be most careful in its allocation of promotional funds. Large sums of money should not be expended during this period for the purpose of expanding total demand. Promotional expenditures should be gauged to the lowest cost combination that will maintain the stability that is typical of the maturity phase.

Professor Stanton summarises the use of personal selling as follows: "Personal selling will carry the bulk of the promotional load (1) when the company is small or has insufficient funds with which to carry on an adequate advertising programme, (2) when the market is concentrated, or (3) when the personality of the salesman is needed to establish rapport or create confidence. Personal selling will also be emphasized when the product (4) has a higher unit value, (5) requires demonstration, (6) must be fitted to the individual customer's needs . . . (7) is purchased infrequently or (8) involves a trade-in."[6]

Planning for Advertising

It becomes more and more a conditioned reflex to say that planning must precede some particular marketing activity. Planning for advertising is no exception. As one becomes familiar with the advertising area, he begins to realize that many of the problems of advertising management are really problems of planning. Without going into detail at this time, it is quite safe to say that a large part of the difficulty in evaluating advertising effectiveness is poor definition of objectives.

The advertising manager's complaint that he cannot possibly choose an optimal media strategy may only be a symptom of his failure to carry out an adequate appraisal of the situation. Advertising departments must carry out their own particular type of audit. Opportunity analysis, consumer research and media research may all be considered part of the advertising planning problem.

Because of its almost infinite complexity, planning in the advertising area becomes highly critical. The advertising plan should be a logical extension of the company's overall marketing plan. It is the statement of marketing strategy that will guide the relationship of advertising to the total marketing mix. The proper establishment of balance in the mix depends on advertising setting its goals with reference to the overall marketing plan and then thoroughly developing its own plan or set of tactics.

---

[6] Op. cit., Stanton, pp. 542-3.

Without a complete advertising plan and the fulfilment of all planning functions, it would be impossible to control the advertising department. "Managerial control must be based on sound criteria both to direct and evaluate advertising activities. Accountability in advertising, for example, should be related to the job advertising is expected to do; . . . careful planning for advertising can provide for management a set of standards and guides . . . essential for control and evaluation."[7]

The need for complete planning in advertising is made more critical by the fact that the advertising plan will determine the advertising appropriation, have direct bearing on the total marketing budget and will affect the total profit picture.

Modern management requires that every expenditure be justified in terms of an expected result. As a result of sophisticated planning, the advertising department can provide management with an intelligent and realistic assessment of opportunity and required expenditure. This information can then be used by marketing management to determine the advertising appropriation. If every section of the marketing department follows this type of planning procedure, marketing management can then make a similarly intelligent assessment of its total budget needs. It seems unnecessary to point out that inadequate planning of the advertising function must automatically lead to sub-optimization of corporate profits.

Finally we can state that planning in advertising is the prerequisite for a logical advertising programme. Proper planning should be directed towards finding the answers to the following questions:

"1. What is the opportunity for profitable advertising?
2. What markets offer greatest potentials?
3. What characteristics of the product lend themselves most profitably to advertising?
4. What motives lie behind consumer decisions to purchase or not to purchase the product?
5. What is the logical market target?
6. What is the specific role of advertising in the promotion programme?
7. What is the role of promotion in the marketing programme?
8. What are the advertising goals of marketing effort?
9. What broad appeals will be most appropriate for accomplishing the advertising objectives?"[8]

Referring back to our early discussions of planning, you will remember we outlined the planning process as follows:

[7] Frey (Ed.), *Marketing Handbook,* Ronald Press, New York, 2nd Ed., 1965, pp. 17.1-2.
[8] Ibid., p. 14.3.

1. Defining Objectives.
2. Developing Planning Assumptions.
3. Collecting Data and Developing Alternatives.
4. Evaluating Alternatives.
5. Selection.

At this stage, we will be concerned with the steps anticedent to the planning of campaigns, which is the phase generally called developing alternatives. We can divide this antecedent into two parts; first is the preliminary fact finding and analysis (advertising audit), second is the establishment of a general control plan (objectives, strategies, budget).

Preliminary fact finding hopes to establish a solid foundation for what must eventually become a highly creative non-quantitative job. Creativity will be the key to developing an adequate advertising campaign. But the directing force in turning the creative key should be a complete factual analysis of the advertising opportunity and its environment. The advertising programme must tie into the marketing programme. Therefore, the advertising executive will want "all major facts about the market, competitive advertising, company resources, product attributes, product mix characteristics, distribution channels, organization and methods for personal selling, existing advertising and sales promotion policy, philosophy and attitude of top management toward advertising."[9] We must not leave out the fact that the advertising department, along with all other departments, must have complete knowledge of current consumers and potential consumers. Frey lists what he considers important pieces of information needed about the product, the consumer and the trend affecting demand. With the preliminary information provided by answers to these questions, the advertising manager can begin to develop his control plan.

"Product.
1. What consumer wants are satisfied by the product?
2. Are the wants strong?
3. Does purchase or use of the product produce any disadvantages to the consumer?
4. What reasons exist to cause prospects to resist buying the product?
5. Can these objections be overcome through advertising?
6. What appeals can be used for advertising the product?
7. Are these appeals strong in motivating consumers?

Consumer Market.
1. Who are present users of the product?

---

9 Op. cit., Alexander, pp. 351-2.

2. What is the size of the present market?
3. Who influences the buying decision?
4. Where is the market located?
5. How often is the product purchased?
6. How much do consumers buy?
7. When do consumers buy?
8. Who are the non-users of the product?
9. What reasons explain their non-purchase?
10. To what extent are non-users prospects for the product?

Consumer Alternatives.

1. What consumer wants compete with those for which this product is purchased?
2. Are competing wants stronger or weaker than those related to the product?
3. What direct alternatives exist for satisfying the same consumer wants that this product satisfies?
4. How do appeals appropriate for the product compare in strength with appeals appropriate for substitute products?

Trend Affecting Demand.

1. Is industry demand for the product expanding?
2. Do social trends favour acceptance of the product?
3. Are environmental trends favourable to the product's acceptance?
4. What are the environmental and social trends affecting substitute products and substitute wants?
5. Can advertising be used to accelerate favourable trends?
6. Where trends are unfavourable, can advertising be expected to substantially retard the trend to produce a reasonable time period for advertising payoff?
7. Can basic causes of social and environmental trends be identified?"[10]

Although he may not be able to get specific and absolute answers to the above questions, the advertising manager will be in a stronger position because of the knowledge gained in searching for the answers.

Let us now look at the traditional starting point in all discussions of planning, (objectives). Formulation of objectives is a process of successive refinement. For example, first corporate objectives are stated; from the corporate objective, marketing management can develop a marketing objective. Carrying on this logical succession, we get marketing objectives leading to advertising objectives, leading to campaign objectives, terminating in the objectives for a single advertisement.

Setting the advertising objective will require the determination

---

10 Op. cit., Frey, pp. 14.7-19.8.

of a planning period, setting specific targets and pinpointing goals. Products moving through their life cycle require different types of advertising in each stage. A company may define each stage in the cycle as an appropriate planning period for advertising. For other products, seasonal or cyclical, time patterns are most important and often act as an advertising planning period. Planning within a particular time period is one way of anticipating changes in advertising needs and meeting their new requirements. A simple rule to follow would be that advertising planning periods should be directly related to the time periods of significant importance to the product. There is no magic in planning by calendar time periods.

One step before setting down the specific advertising goals is identification of the advertising target. Although we talk of advertising as being mass communication, there is, or should be, a specific group of individuals identified as the target. Advertising targets can be potential customers, opinion leaders or gatekeepers. Part of target identification involves a decision between "push" and "pull" philosophies. "Pull" type advertising aims at the final customer and depends on him building up demand pressure strong enough to influence channel members to purchase. "Push" advertising is aimed at the middleman and hopes to stimulate his pulling the item through the channel structure. Once the target is identified, the job of setting specific objectives or goals can be started.

Advertising goals, no less than corporate goals, should be clear, unambiguous statements of the advertising purpose. They should be directly related to marketing goals and corporate goals. Every part of the advertising programme, down to the smallest individual advertisement, should have a specific objective whose achievement will help meet the corporate objectives.

Perhaps the most difficult part of planning an advertising control system is establishing the advertising appropriation or budget. There are many techniques suggested from various sources on how to determine the advertising appropriation. We will quickly look at each method.

1. Fixed percentage or percentage of sales.
2. Competitive matching.
3. Available funds.
4. Objective—task.
5. Marginal revenue approach.
6. Marketing approach.

Fixed Percentage Method: This method says that the advertising budget should be some fixed percentage of last year's sales or anticipated sales. There is little sound logical reasoning that can be used to defend this method. In periods of declining sales, this method could lead to a reduction of advertising expenditure when the opposite is necessary. Fixed percentage methods seem to be saying that advertising is the result of sales when we at least hope that advertising is the partial cause of sales. The widespread acceptance of the method seems to be based on the comparative ease of its use and the fact that it is relatively safe. In simple terms, it always picks a volume of advertising that the company can afford.

Competitive Matching: The competitive matching approach says that your advertising budget should be equal to the competition's if you want an equal market share. This method assumes there is a direct relation between advertising expenditure and share of market. Competitive matching is defended as a method of protection against severe competitive inroads. In the final analysis, there seems to be only limited validity to this approach.

Available Funds: Available funds methods say that all that is possibly available should be allocated to advertising. Where there is a strong immediate cause and effect relationship between expenditure and sales, the available funds method may be defended. Because there is usually a time lag between the expenditure and advertising results, the available-funds method can easily cause financial embarrassment. It can also lead to the stopping of a campaign at a crucial period because of the lack of immediate liquidity.

Objective and Task: This method is based on the assumption that the advertising budget is simply a function of the job to be done. "The actual method is based on finding the answers to four questions: (1) What do we want to accomplish, and what is the dollar value of each of our advertising objectives? (2) What tasks must be performed by advertising and sales promotion to achieve each objective? (3) What will it cost to perform these tasks? (4) Are these costs less than the estimated value of the objectives to which they relate, and do we have sufficient money to cover them?"[11] If the firm carefully evaluates the value of achieving any specific objective, there is little basic fault with the objective and task method. Its greatest shortcoming is that it does not re-evaluate each advertising objective

---

11 Op. cit., Alexander, p. 364.

with reference to the total marketing plan. We will discuss this point in more detail when we cover the marketing programme approach.

Marginal Revenue Approach: The idea behind this method is simple. First, the relationship between sales and advertising is established. Various sales-profit relationships are looked at and the point of optimality is determined. If one could easily establish the relationship between advertising and sales, the marginal revenue or incremental approach is easy. In the pure situation, where advertising is the only, or at least, major promotional activity, the marginal approach can be justified. As a theoretical approach, the method cannot be attacked as it guarantees maximum profit. As a practical matter, the method leaves a great deal to be desired.

Marketing Programme: Advertising is only one part of a complete marketing programme. Its appropriation cannot be established in a relative vacuum that only sets the advertising objective once. The advertising objective is a strict function of the cost involved in achieving it. As the cost of achieving any specific objective is determined, it must be related to the costs of achieving the result with all other possible combinations of the marketing mix. What we are emphasizing at this point is that the marketing mix is a closed system which can exist in many combinations. The final relationship between each part of the mix should be designed to optimize profit. In practice, the marketing programme approach is a combination of the objective and task method and marginal revenue approaches. Its basic refinement is that it provides a unifying concept.

One must realize that we have discussed setting the appropriation before the design of any specific campaign. Again the discussion of objectives and budget was placed first as an expedient. One could not set any final operating objective or control budget until a final campaign or set of campaigns had been designed.

Copy and Media Strategy

If one accepts the initial premise that advertising accomplishes its objectives through communication and the process of learning, he would then start any study of campaign strategy with a review of these two areas. While no one can claim to have the final answers on how and why certain communications are more effective, we can look to a fair amount of communications and learning theory for guidance.

159

Marketing: the Management Way

In 1955, Professor Steuart Henderson Britt wrote an article in which he listed twenty principles of learning which have meaning for advertising. They are given below without comment, leaving you to draw your own conclusions.

"1. Unpleasant things may sometimes be learned as readily as pleasant things, but the most ineffective stimuli are those which arouse little or no emotional response. . . .

2. The capacities of learners are important in determining what can be learned and how long it will take. . . .

3. Things that are learned and understood tend to be better retained than things learned by rote. . . .

4. Practice distributed over several periods is more economical in learning than the same amount of practice concentrated into a single period. . . .

5. When teaching people to master mechanical skills, it is better to show the performance in the same way that the learner would see it if he were doing the job himself. . . .

6. The order of presentation of materials to be learned is very important. Points presented at the beginning and end of the message are remembered better than those in the middle. . . .

7. If material to be learned is different, or unique, it will be better remembered.

8. Showing errors in how to do something can lead to increases in learning.

9. Learning situations which are rewarded only occasionally can be more effective than those where constant reward is employed. . . .

10. It is easier to recognize something than it is to recall it.

11. The rate of forgetting tends to be very rapid immediately after learning. . .

12. Messages attributed to persons held in high esteem influence change in opinion more than messages from persons not so well-known, but after several weeks both messages seem equally effective. . . .

13. Repetition of identical materials is often as effective in getting things remembered as repeating the same story, but with variations. . . .

14. In a learning situation, a moderate fear appeal is more effective than a strong fear appeal. . . .

15. Knowledge of results leads to increases in learning. . . .

16. Learning is aided by active practice rather than passive reception. . . .

17. A message is more easily learned and accepted if it does not interfere with earlier habits. . . .

18. The mere repetition of a situation does not necessarily lead to learning. Two things are necessary—'belongingness,' and 'satisfiers' . . .

160

19. When two ideas are of equal strength but of unequal age, new repetition increases the strength of the earlier idea more than that of the newer idea.
20. Learning something new can interfere with the remembering of something learned earlier."[12]

We also know a good deal about the human factor which affects the effectiveness of a communication. For communication to be called successful, four conditions must be met. The audience must be "exposed" to the communication correctly, the audience must receive the message correctly, the audience must "retain" the basic idea of the message and finally, the audience must "decide" whether or not to act on the communication. The process by which an audience member decides to receive a message is called selective exposure, selective perception, selective retention and selective decision.

Research has shown that people tend to expose themselves to communications in which they are interested or which tend to conform to their existing attitudes. We also tend to avoid communications that are irritating, uninteresting or incompatible with our previous opinions. When exposed to a communication, we will tend to perceive it in a way that will support our own predisposition. Retention of compatible ideas is stronger and more long-lasting than retention of ideas that are incompatible. Finally, there is evidence that suggests even when a message is perceived correctly and retained, it will not be acted upon if it contradicts a previous attitude.

The warning for advertisers in these findings is obvious. For an advertisement to change a strongly held attitude it must fight through an almost impenetrable set of obstacles. We do not mean to discourage all advertisers from trying to change consumer attitudes. What is hoped is that you will realize how much more difficult it is to change rather than reinforce an attitude. Possibly, we can draw the conclusion that when attempting to change consumer attitudes, we do it within a framework that is familiar and acceptable to the consumer. What we are suggesting is that messages to change attitude should be encased in a setting that is acceptable to the audience.

John C. Maloney, manager of Research Development, Leo Burnett Company, in an article entitled "Is Advertising Believability Really Important?", lists ten conclusions to be drawn from research into communications. We reproduce these conclusions without comment.

---

12 "How Advertising Can Use Psychology's Rules of Learning," *Printers Ink,* Sept. 23, 1955, Printers Ink Pub. Co.

Ten Conclusions

"Here are ten important conclusions to be drawn:

"1. Different consumers bring different beliefs, interests, and attitudes to an advertisement; and an advertisement which is believable to some people will not be believable to others. To evaluate the belief of advertising, one must know *who* should believe and *what* should be believed in terms of the advertiser's intentions.

"2. Consumers' already existing beliefs or attitudes relate to many separate stages of believing advertisements. As a preliminary to belief, the consumer must focus attention upon the advertisement once he is exposed to it. In doing this, he makes a very general 'what-this-is-all-about' judgement of the advertisement. At this early stage, the advertisement loses any chances of being believed unless it somehow relates to previously developed beliefs, interests, or attitudes.

"3. Once the consumer focuses attention on an advertisement, the advertising message must find its way to the consumer's already existing attitudes *toward the product* without being side-tracked. Too often the advertising message is 'misindexed' at this stage because: (a) it is too 'addy' and simply reminds the consumer of advertising rather than the product; (b) it is too remindful of competitors' products or services; or (c) it starts a chain of thoughts about irrelevant attention-getting devices in the advertising.

"4. Once the advertisement is seen as being germane to the consumer's way of looking at the product or service, the main impediment to belief is unconscious distortion of the intended meaning of the advertising message. In order to make the meaning of the message fit in with his old attitudes, the consumer may 'level' the message, overlooking parts of the message with which he disagrees; or he may 'sharpen' the message, adding certain meanings to the advertisement which the advertiser had not really intended. In either case, the distortion of the message meaning precludes any chance of belief. ('Sharpening' *sometimes* works to the advertisers' advantage *if* the consumers' attitude toward the product is already favourable.)

"5. If the consumer focuses attention on the advertisement, indexes it properly and does not distort its meaning, he may believe the advertising message only temporarily. There are two main reasons that much apparent belief of advertising fails to hold up over time. One is the simple fact that consumers cannot or will not remember all the things about a product that advertisers might like them to remember. Second, much belief of advertising is tentative belief, not sufficiently well supported by the consumer's earlier experiences or previously developed attitudes. Such tentative belief will fade unless there is early support from future experiences with the product, repeated exposure to similar advertising or word-of-mouth advertising.

"6. No single advertisement is likely to be believed completely if belief requires the consumer to change his mind about the product. Unless the consumer is already 'sold' on a product, complete belief in new products, involving 'adoption' of them, may take months or even years.

"7. Advertising is especially effective for making people aware of, interested in, *or curious about* new or improved products; and thus advertising is a very effective aid to developing *tentative belief* in a product. While advertising also helps to induce trial of the product, complete belief in the product's merits usually requires that the selling messages be supported by sales personnel, and the comments or examples of family members or acquaintances.

"8. Within the groups of people to whom consumers look for example and guidance in making product or brand choices, there is a minority of people who are especially interested in the product class. These 'opinion leaders' often relay advertising messages to others or reinforce the 'believability' of these messages for others—by example or by word of mouth. Thus, there often tends to be a 'two-step flow' of advertising influence—from the advertising to 'opinion leaders,' and from 'opinion leaders' to 'opinion followers.'

"It is sometimes to the advertiser's advantage to cater to the 'opinion leaders' and to capitalize upon the 'two-step flow' of advertising influence. Sometimes, however, the advertiser is better off to ignore the potential 'opinion leaders' and to short-circuit the 'two-step flow' of advertising. The latter course of action is no doubt best when the consumer feels little risk in believing in the product or service, that is, when he can make a brand choice without feeling any need to depend upon the guidance of others.

"9. The advertiser must always be concerned about having his message noticed; and consumers should be able to recognize easily that the message relates to the advertised product in a way that is relevant to their own needs or interests. However, the advertiser need not be too concerned about advertising messages which 'sound too good to be true' *if* the consumer has a real opportunity to find out that they *are* true.

"10. Finally, the advertiser must remember that the most persuasive advertising messages are those which are most congruent with the consumer's experiences, both past and future. And it is not just the consumer's experience of seeing, hearing, or reading advertisements that matters.

"One-at-a-time advertising exposures do not account for belief

163

by themselves. ALL BELIEVABLE ADVERTISING IS, TO SOME DEGREE, 'REMINDER ADVERTISING'."[13]

Media Selection Problems

Compounding the advertiser's problems almost beyond comprehension is the media selection dilemma. Assuming that the media selected to present a communication should be optimized, we assume ourselves into a horrible problem. Let us take a brief look at some of the detailed information needed to make a rational and theoretically optimal media decision. First, it goes without saying that you must have complete demographic, economic and sociological data about consumers and potential consumers. You will want to know purchasing habits of consumers, including brand switching probabilities. Important amongst the purchase information is rate of purchase data. For application of most sophisticated solutions to the media problem, brand-share information is required.

Specific information is needed for every possible media selection. At a minimum, information on audience size, audience composition, rate structure and exposure should be sought.

If the advertiser could obtain all the information he needed to make an optimal choice of media, he would most certainly need a computer to reach a solution. Young and Rubican have developed a media selection model and in Figure Five, opposite, we present the block diagram outlining its use.[14]

There are many practical day to day problems in media selection that are beyond the scope of this discussion. For readers more interested in the detail of media selection, Brown, ed., *Advertising Media,* Ronald Press, is suggested.

Evaluation of Advertising Expenditure

Evaluation of advertising expenditure simply adds to the difficulty of advertising management. After one struggles through the problems of developing campaign strategy and arriving at a final media selection, there is no sure way for measuring success. Because of the basic lack of a directly measurable relationship between sales and advertising and because of ignorance of how advertising works, many varied measures of success have developed. We will look at five

[13] "Is Advertising Believability Really Important?", *Journal of Marketing,* Vol. 27, Oct., 1963, Maloney, J. C.. Reprinted from the *Journal of Marketing,* pp. 7-8, national quarterly publication of the American Marketing Association.

[14] *Practical Media Decisions and the Computer,* William T. McRaw, Journal of Marketing, Vol. 27, July, 1963. Reprinted from the *Journal of Marketing,* national quarterly publication of the American Marketing Association.

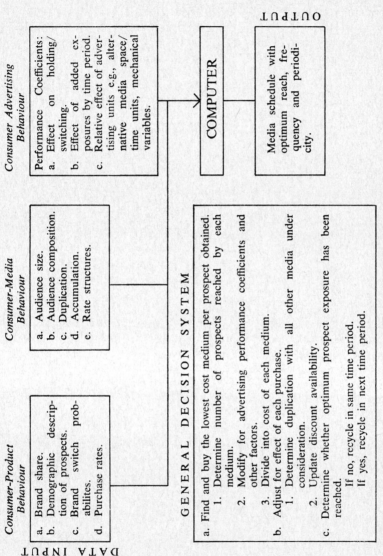

COMPUTER

Media schedule with optimum reach, frequency and periodicity.

Consumer Advertising Behaviour

Performance Coefficients:
a. Effect on holding/switching.
b. Effect of added exposures by time period.
c. Relative effect of advertising units e.g., alternative media space/time units, mechanical variables.

Consumer-Media Behaviour

a. Audience size.
b. Audience composition.
c. Duplication.
d. Accumulation.
e. Rate structures.

Consumer-Product Behaviour

a. Brand share.
b. Demographic description of prospects.
c. Brand switch probabilities.
d. Purchase rates.

GENERAL DECISION SYSTEM

a. Find and buy the lowest cost medium per prospect obtained.
   1. Determine number of prospects reached by each medium.
   2. Modify for advertising performance coefficients and other factors.
   3. Divide into cost of each medium.
b. Adjust for effect of each purchase.
   1. Determine duplication with all other media under consideration.
   2. Update discount availability.
c. Determine whether optimum prospect exposure has been reached.
   If no, recycle in same time period.
   If yes, recycle in next time period.

FIGURE FIVE

general classes of evaluation techniques: Recognition Tests, Recall Tests, Opinion and Attitude Ratings, Projective Methods, Inquiries and Sales Measures.

Recognition Tests: Recognition tests in their pure form purport to measure what part of an audience will recognize that they have seen a particular advertisement when they are exposed to it under test conditions. The procedure works something as follows: A respondent is asked if they have seen a particular magazine and if they have read through it. If yes, the interviewer goes through the magazine with the respondent asking if he recalls seeing particular advertisements. Some testing schemes break down the recognition scores into "noted", "seen/associated" and "read most". Advertising recognition tests are carried out by many firms; the most famous, and also a pioneer in the field, is Daniel Starch.

Advertising recognition tests are filled with many technical problems. Some of the problems faced by the researcher are involved with learning how to deal with the following: "Genuine confusion with other advertising, guessing when uncertain, deliberate exaggeration, deduction that advertisement was seen based on recognition of surrounding material, deduction of likely noting, based on memory or knowledge of one's own reading habits, eagerness to please the interviewer, hesitation to appear ignorant . . ."[15] Other problems are created by variations in thickness of issue, position of the advertisement in the issue or the interview, and variations in interviewing staff.

Advertising researchers have long had serious doubts about recognition testing as a method of measuring advertising effectiveness. There are serious doubts about the statistical validity of the tests. There is even doubt if the current testing methods measure recognition. Finally the advertising manager may question the usefulness of knowing what percentage of an audience remembers that it saw his advertisement.

With all their shortcomings, we might ask ourselves why recognition tests are so popular. First in importance is that a properly designed recognition test measures something that the ad has done under normal conditions. The testing method can test real advertisements under real conditions. Closely allied is the fact that recognition tests measure a physical reality rather than an opinion. Finally, the cost of this type of research is comparatively low.

---

[15] Britt & Lucas, *Measuring Advertising Effectiveness*, McGraw-Hill Book Co., New York, 1963, p. 60.

Recall Tests: Recall testing carries the recognition test one step further. It says it is most important that the audience member who claims to have seen an advertisement should be able to tell you something about the ad. The testing procedure is as follows: The interviewer locates people who claim to have read a particular magazine. The members of the audience are then shown a list of names of logotypes of all advertisements in the particular magazine. Certain of the names are fictitious and the respondent is sometimes given this information. From the list of names, the respondent is asked which he remembers seeing in that issue. Once the repondent says he saw a particular ad he is asked to tell something about its content. In addition to all the problems of recognition testing, the recall test has the problem of defining between adequate and inadequate recall.

Under good conditions the recall test can be used to measure the media memorability, communication and comprehension. With a properly designed sample, it is possible to get some degree of statistical validity in a recall test. Recall tests have been used with some degree of success for radio and television audiences, in addition to audiences of printed media.

In general, it is almost impossible to go from recall and recognition data to success of an advertisement in producing sales. If one assumes that an advertisement must be recognized and recalled before it can do its job, then these tests serve some specific control purpose. Some advertisers now use recognition and recall tests to pre-test particular advertisements. There seems to be some validity in using the recall test as a preliminary screening device.

Opinion and Attitude Ratings: Ask a person his opinion of an advertisement and he will tell you. That is the basis for opinion and attitude ratings in advertising testing. Asking the correct people the correct questions are the critical portions of turning opinion testing from an interesting game into a meaningful experiment.

The earliest experiments in opinion and attitude testing took the form of exposing a person to an advertisement and asking him if he thought the ad was good. He might then be asked if he thought the advertisement would stimulate his purchase of the item. After several years of this kind of testing, researchers realized a different type of attack was needed to get meaningful answers. The audience evaluation of whether an advertisement was good proved of little value and there was little validity in customer predictions of future behaviour.

167

The next phase of opinion testing took the form of asking the respondent questions like: "Is the advertisement interesting to you? Do you believe the ad?" In other words, the respondent was asked how the advertisement affected him with regard to characteristics that the advertiser felt important.

While the validity of this type of opinion testing has been difficult to prove, the method is widespread as a pre-introduction testing method.

Several other methods of opinion testing have been developed. One is called the indirect method. In this type of testing, the respondent is told he will receive a gift for participating in an experiment. He is then permitted to identify his choice of gift from a selection of items. Once the gift has been identified, the respondent is shown what is supposed to be a pilot test of a new television programme. The television programme includes advertising, and, specifically, advertising for one of the gift items available for choice. After the respondent watches the television programme, he is allowed to make his gift choice again. The change in popularity of the advertised product is then taken as a gauge of the advertisement's effectiveness.

There have been many refinements in opinion testing over the years. Sophisticated scaling and rating techniques have been developed. Paired comparison tests have become popular. If one realizes that there are shortcomings in taking the opinions of potential customers as a guide to advertising effectiveness and if one realizes that all he can possibly get from an opinion test is a broad rough comparison, then there is a place for opinion testing as a method of pre-testing advertisements.

Projective Methods: We have covered various projective techniques in an earlier discussion of motivation research. Let us now just look at how three different techniques might be used to evaluate an advertisement. We will look at word association, sentence completion and picture techniques.

In the word association test, the advertiser takes the words in his advertisement he thinks are image forming and then tests them for their particular image. If his advertisement contains ten image forming words, the advertiser may take these ten words, along with ten other words, and make the twenty words into a meaningless list. The respondent is then asked to tell or write the first word that comes to mind as he sees each word in the list.

There is a very valid reason for this type of testing. Everyone brings their own set of prejudices to the interpretation of a word's meaning. If a significant portion of a population misperceives a word's meaning, then it should quickly be dropped from the ad. Word association tests are supposed to tell us how a person perceives a particular word.

Sentence completion tests are ideally suited for testing important phrases in a piece of copy. In the test, a person would be given the first part of an advertising slogan and would then be asked to complete the sentence. We could use this type of test to see what chain of thinking the introductory phrases in an advertisement stimulated. We might also use actual in-use advertisements to see if the advertisement has been memorized.

The sentence completion test may be used to test how effectively an advertisement's message has gone across. In this case, a respondent would be exposed to an advertisement. He would then be given a series of sentences to complete. These sentences would relate in some way to the advertisement he had been exposed to.

Picture techniques simply show a respondent the art work in an advertisement and then ask the respondent to tell what is happening in the advertisement. It is hoped that this will reveal how the person reacts to the advertisement.

Again, one must be very careful before accepting or rejecting the various projection techniques as tests of advertising effectiveness. No one to date has been able to relate supposedly good reactions on projection techniques to high sales produced by the advertisement. At best, we can hope to get clues about what reaction an advertisement is apt to generate. We certainly cannot predict what sales the advertisement will generate from a projection technique.

Inquiries and Sales Measures: Certain forms of advertising allow for direct evaluation of their sales effectiveness. Firms that depend 100% on mail order advertising can easily judge the relative merits of different copy formats in producing sales. Some advertisers use only radio or television to solicit inquiries. This method also allows comparison of various copy formats. The return coupon has been used to measure the relative effectiveness of various advertisements. Coupon methods lack any true validity if their results are used to state the effectiveness of future advertisements that do not contain a coupon.

What does the advertiser do when he does not want to use a coupon, but yet he wants to be able to judge the sales production of his advertising? If the manager insists on measuring the effectiveness of single advertisements, there is little he can hope for in the way of accurate measurement. If, on the other hand, the manager is willing to look at an entire campaign, he does have some hope of success. You will notice we have made a shift in emphasis at this point. We are no longer looking for a predictor of advertising effectiveness but rather a post-operative evaluator of effectiveness. Before leaving the matter of predicting advertising effectiveness, we should conclude that there is not now any single method that can and should be used as the sole evaluator of the possible effectiveness of a piece of copy.

The method that seems to hold most promise for performing post-operative advertising analysis is some type of correlation analysis. Most of the straightforward correlation analysis between advertising and sales response has been unprofitable. Researchers seem to forget that there is a time lag effect in advertising and also an inertia type of effect.

If one takes time lag and inertia into consideration, he stands a good chance of building a reliable correlation analysis. What is necessary is that an estimate must be made about the total time in which an advertisement is effective. Then an estimate must be made about how this effectiveness is distributed. For example, assume you have an ad that seems to be effective or at least remembered for four months. You must then estimate how to divide the 100% of advertising effectiveness over the four months. Again, as an example, you may decide that 20% of the advertisement's effect takes place in the first month and 40, 30 and 10% in the 2nd, 3rd and 4th months respectively.

After making these estimates, each month's total advertising expenditure would be distributed according to the percentages in your time pattern of effectiveness. Realising that one cannot easily assign these percentages, it is suggested that a computer be used to run many simulations and to pick the one that creates the best correlation.

The above method is described in detail by Robert J. Williams in an article entitled "The Relation Between Advertising Pressure and Consumer Sales." This article appears in the Irwin publication, *Advertising Management*. For those who are interested in this general area, it is suggested that you read the Williams article.

Conclusions on Evaluating Advertising Effectiveness

It seems unrewarding to come to the end of a discussion on evaluating the effectiveness of advertising and not being able

170

to draw any positive conclusions. We have found many interesting techniques for pre-testing and post-testing various characteristics of advertisements. We do not yet have a way of going to a statement of cause and effect between advertisement and sales. These problems do not mean the advertising manager should not be using any criteria for evaluating his output. What it does mean is that for the time being we cannot attach a 100% certainty between any particular measure of advertising effectiveness and sales. But we can relate many of the things necessary for a sale to a particular advertisement. These things, such as exposure, recall and attitude, are all necessary for a sale to take place and we are making rapid progress in the measurement of these factors.

One final remark must be made on evaluating advertising effectiveness. Effectiveness must always be measured against an objective. We have assumed throughout most of our discussion that sales were the objective of an advertisement. If we make assumptions such as advertising's objective being the creation of awareness or creating comprehension, then many of the cause and effect arguments presented are not meaningful. It is the type of reasoning that says advertising has many objectives leading to a sale that causes the acceptance of such things as recall and recognition tests. We are by no means prepared to say that this type of reasoning is invalid. We must only be prepared for the eventuality that advertisements that score high in the sub-objectives of recall, recognition, good opinion and high interest may not produce profitable sales.

Client-Advertising Agency Relationship

At this point we do not wish to go into any long discussion of the formalities in client-agency relationships. Our only wish is to bring out several important concepts.

When an advertising agency is entrusted with your product, it is entrusted in large part with your company's life. If the agency misinterprets your corporate goals and objectives and if it does not understand what you want to accomplish with the particular product, it can do much more harm than good. The agency must be considered as an extension of the client's company. It must be privileged to the types of information that tell why a company is in business and what it hopes to accomplish. It must not be considered as an outsider doing its job in an atmosphere other than the atmosphere of the client company.

For this type of relationship to develop, it must be built on

171

a sound foundation. This foundation requires a solid feeling of permanence of relationship. If either client or agency feels any hesitation about the permanence of the relationship, there cannot be an effective exchange of ideas.

What we are saying is that the client agency relationship must be a mature, intelligent relationship. There must be freedom for exchange of ideas. There cannot be a constant fear that the agency is encroaching on the marketing department's area of interest, nor can the marketing department run the advertising agency. Each party must realize its responsibility to each other and each must be willing to listen to criticism from the other. The agency-client relationship stands the best chance of success when each party realizes its mutual dependence.

General Conclusions

Our discussion of advertising has covered a large amount of material. We have not dealt in detail with any specific area. Perhaps the only general conclusion we can reach is that advertising can, and should be, subject to management control. There are problems of measurement and evaluation, but these problems do not prohibit a managerial approach to the advertising function. Advertising spends far too much money to be allowed to function with imprecise definition of objectives and ineffective planning of programmes.

DISCUSSION QUESTIONS

1. What factors seem to affect the opportunity to advertise effectively?
2. What part does planning play in advertising management?
3. What information is necessary to make intelligent advertising decisions?
4. Discuss the relative merits of the various techniques used to measure advertising effectiveness.
5. How should advertising allocation be determined?

BIBLIOGRAPHY

BORDEN: *The Economic Effects of Advertising*, Richard D. Irwin Inc., Homewood, Ill., U.S.A.

BOYD & NEWMAN (Ed.): *Advertising Management*, Richard D. Irwin Inc., Homewood, Ill., U.S.A.

BRITT: "How Advertising Can Use Psychology's Rules of Learning", *Printer's Ink*, Printer's Ink Publishing Co., New York, N.Y., U.S.A.

BRITT & LUCAS: *Measuring Advertising Effectiveness*, McGraw-Hill, New York, N.Y., U.S.A.

FREY: *Advertising*, Ronald Press, New York, N.Y., U.S.A.

FREY (Ed.): *Marketing Handbook*, Ronald Press, New York, N.Y., U.S.A.

MALONEY: "Is Advertising Believability Really Important?" *Journal of Marketing*, Vol. 27, Chicago, Ill., U.S.A.

McRAW: "Practical Media Decisions and the Computer", *Journal of Marketing*, Vol. 27, 1963, Chicago, Ill., U.S.A.

10

Sales Planning
and Control

A COMPLETE study of all problems connected with sales management would cover sales planning and control and administration. Sales planning and control, the first area, is concerned with such things as the sales programme, determination of sales potential, the establishment of territories and finally, sales analysis and evaluation. Administration, while no less important, is concerned with such things as selection of salesmen, training, compensation and supervision. We have not covered the administrative problems in any other area of marketing and for this reason we will not cover the administrative problems in our discussion of sales planning and control.

Our discussion of the planning and control functions will be fairly detailed but of limited scope. As an introduction, we will look at the sales management job and analyse how it has been changing over the years. Coverage of planning and control will start with a look at the sales programme. We will then move on to an analysis of sales potential. Our purpose will be to show the importance of knowing sales potential. Next, we will look at the actual areas of analysis and evaluation. Our interest will be in developing an organized approach to the evaluation of product sales, customer importance, sales costs and sales force performance.

As the final part of our planning and control discussion, we will show how sales analysis helps to solve the problems of territory boundaries and determination of how many salesmen are necessary.

174

Changing Character of the Sales Management Job

With corporate acceptance of the marketing concept, the sales and sales management jobs change in scope and character. Salesmen are encouraged to think of their job as one part of the total effort necessary to achieve the corporate objective. Sales management is called upon to integrate its managerial effort into the total marketing complex.

During the stage of corporate development called "Sales Orientation", the salesman was simply the seller of either goods or services. He had little regard for overall corporate objectives and very little understanding of their importance. At this stage of development, the salesman usually restricted his work to selling the products currently offered by his company. To request the salesman's further participation in the marketing process would not even occur to management. The marketing job or the sales job at this time in history was regarded as a necessary antecedent for moving the corporate production.

Today the salesman has a vastly different function. He is involved with every step of the distribution process. The salesman becomes involved at the product development stage and remains involved through the period of post delivery service. While his primary responsibility is still selling, the salesman is also responsible for meeting the needs of his customers.

One victim, if you may call him a victim, in this changing sales philosophy has been the sales manager. Before the acceptance of the marketing concept, the sales manager was the top-ranking marketing executive. He usually reported directly to the senior operating manager of the company. Today the sales manager is likely to report to the marketing manager. He may even report to a product manager who has responsibility for the co-ordination of product research, advertising and personal selling.

Although the marketing concept narrows the sales manager's scope of responsibility, it does not make his job any easier. If anything, the sales management job has become more difficult. Looking back to the requirements of the marketing concept, we see that the sales manager must plan all of his activities, he must integrate his activities with the rest of the marketing team, he must utilize research to make his decisions, he must justify all of his activities in terms of corporate objectives. To a man who for many years was his own boss and whose philosophy was simply to increase sales volume, the marketing concept has

175

had many ramifications. For those sales managers who were able to see the value of the marketing concept, the changes in their jobs have been accepted as well as the challenge of their new responsibilities.

The Sales Programme

Because the sales manager's job revolves around his sales programme, we will spend some time looking at its development. Successful sales programmes are the result of many hours of hard work. They require the co-ordinated effort of every member of the marketing team. Sales programmes are the tactical manoeuvres through which the personal selling portion of the total corporate strategy is implemented. The sales programme is simply the step by step outline of personal selling activities that guide a product from producer to consumer.

Marketing strategies are the necessary antecedents to the implementation of sales programmes. Every sales programme must have a core idea or strategic foundation. Generation of strategies, while basically an art, can be aided by the use of some simple tools.

A company's current marketing plan exists within a particular strategic mould. This mould provides the limits to which any factor within the marketing mix can be varied. In an attempt to develop new strategies or to review older strategies, the manager must clearly define the limits of his current mould. Once defined, these limits can be stretched and compressed to find the point where their manipulation prevents profitable marketing. What one is looking for here is a definition of how much freedom he has to manipulate the development of marketing strategies.

With each factor of the marketing mix set within boundaries of action, the elimination process can be started. Freedom of action with certain factors will be so limited that even actions at the extremes will have no effect on the market place. This type of factor can then be excluded from any further consideration. Those factors that remain adjustable after analysis are all candidates for launching new marketing strategies.

The remaining factors in the marketing mix should now be thoroughly analysed and the results of their variation determined. Certain alternative actions will rule themselves out quickly because of violent competitive reaction. After separate consideration of each alternative, you can start to compare various alternatives in terms of achieving corporate objectives. When the list of possible alternatives is reduced to two or three broad strategies, small variations can be tested for significance. Final choice of the strategy may ultimately be reduced to an intuitive decision.

A second method for generating strategies starts with a listing of assumptions that govern present marketing actions. Certain marketing practices may have been started for reasons which no longer exist. Reflecting on how a business would be run if it were starting new with new procedures and assumptions will possibly reveal new strategies.

Most firms enter business because they expect to have some unique advantage in product or service. In looking for new strategies, one should question whether his firm's original competitive advantage has remained or if market changes have altered the situation. "The net competitive advantage of any firm consists of some combination of distinctive features of its products and services, of its technological advantages in production and physical handling of goods and the geographical advantage of location. This bundle of advantages must be reconsidered from time to time as the basis for new and more effective marketing strategies."[1]

Fruitful areas for examination would be neglected markets, unutilized capacity and unrealized economies of scale. Markets that were once unprofitable may be ripe for new strategies. Unutilized capacity can exist in forms other than plant and machinery. Excess capacity within the community may be all that is necessary for a new idea to be successful. Excess population or other firms with seasonal employment patterns may provide new types and sources of labour. Economies of scale may allow for a new marketing strategy. Sales force economies may allow for a new pattern, or increased profit may allow for a change in advertising media.

Competition will often provide clues to alternative strategies. Each competitor has his particular strength or weakness. Every firm is vulnerable to attack on some basis. Creative analysis of competitive firms will often show new marketing opportunities to exist.

We have not mentioned any technique for developing a specific sales programme. Because the sales programme exists as an integral part of a marketing programme, its development grows or comes about as part of the marketing programme.

---

[1] Op. cit., Alderson & Green, p. 458.

Co-ordinating the Sales Programme

The search for a marketing strategy should end with a fully developed statement of objectives. Each factor of the marketing mix where a competitive advantage can be developed should be reviewed. A final statement may be as follows: Leaving all other portions of the marketing mix unchanged, we will hire ten additional salesmen and provide our customers with more specialized service. Another possibility would be to change all factors within the mix from essentially defensive to offensive manoeuvres.

With the statement of objectives as a guide, the specific programme or schedule can be laid out. The three essential elements of the programme are sequence, schedule and budget. The sequence puts each necessary activity in its proper order. A schedule relates the activities to a specific calendar time. The budget relates the sequence of activities to the resources which have been mobilized.

The construction of a sequence is most easily accomplished by working backward from a desired end result and putting in every step which is regarded as a necessary antecedent for the end result or any of its antecedents. This process will show the logical progression of steps necessary to accomplish the task.

Sequence manipulation offers a means of testing the sequence just designed. "When a tentative sequence has been constructed, the planner raises four questions to test it for optimality. He takes the sequence to be optimal when he can no longer improve it by invoking any of the test questions . . .

1. Can any step be eliminated because it turns out that it is not truly a necessary antecedent and because it has detrimental effects on some of the steps which follow?
2. Even though a step is a necessary antecedent to the end result, can it be postponed to a later point in the sequence, thereby avoiding detrimental effects on steps which would otherwise follow it?
3. Can any additional steps be added which would have an instrumental effect on late steps without increasing either the total elapsed time or total cost?
4. Can any step be advanced in the sequence in such a way as to reduce the costs or the elapsed time of steps which would otherwise precede it?"[2]

The most effective tool developed for handling the sequencing problem has been P.E.R.T. or critical path scheduling.

[2] Ibid., p. 477.

Evaluating the Programme in Action

Logical sequencing has been emphasized so far in this discussion. Evaluating the sales programme should continue this process. Sales programme evaluation can take place in two distinct time periods. The programme can be evaluated before its installation or it can be evaluated while it is in action. Evaluation before installation would be the ideal. Unfortunately this type of analysis is still in its infancy. Our current discussion will be limited to evaluation techniques used when the plan is in action.

Planning sales activities begins with a statement of market potential. Sales forecasts should not be developed without some idea of total market potential. When establishing territories or sales quotas, the total market potential of each area should be considered. Analysis of market potential is a complex and specialized job. It is the rare sales manager who is qualified and has the time to carry out his own market research.

As an introduction to sales analysis, we will present a detailed example of how a company can measure sales potential and market penetration. The example shows how a company can gather a crude index of its performance. After the example we will discuss ways of refining this initial data into a meaningful management tool.

An Example in Measuring Sales Potential and Market Penetration

Today, effective marketing demands a readily available means of measuring sales potential and market penetration. New techniques in potential analysis allow the pinpointing of geographic areas where sales are behind precisely set standards of performance. With limited tools, it is possible to calculate the answers to questions such as:

1. What is a reasonable estimate of total sales potential?
2. What is a reasonable estimate of individual territory sales potential?
3. Which sales territories are getting the most "mileage" from available business?
4. Which territories are lagging behind and are in need of special attention?

While the exact procedures in any sales analysis will vary with the specific situation, there are five fundamental steps that remain similar in all cases.

1. Determining the distribution of the company's sales according to important customer classifications.

179

2. Calculating a common expression with which to identify potential.
3. Calculating potential for desired geographic areas.
4. Deriving performance figures.
5. Making the final analysis and determining total company sales potential.

STEP ONE

For illustration purposes, this example will be assuming a firm that sells industrial products. The basic concepts are equally as relevant to firms selling consumer products.

Most state and federal governments have assigned industrial code numbers to firms within specific industries. In the United States this number is called the Standard Industrial Classification (S.I.C.). The Australian equivalent of the S.I.C. is called a factory class number. These classification numbers make it possible to classify customers according to a uniformly accepted system of industrial identification.

Assign classification numbers to each company that has purchased from you in the past four years. After assigning classification numbers, group customers by industrial classification. Then, total the value of customer purchases by classification group for the past four years. Next, calculate the percentage of business that came from each industry group.

Many companies doing business in industrial markets lose the identity of their final customers because sales are made through independent distributors. The identity of these customers must be regained. It can be done by attaching a post-paid reply card to each item shipped to a distributor. Ask him to fill in the purchasing company's name, address and business as he sells the product. In this way it is possible to find the value of distributor sales going to particular industry groups.

STEP TWO

The industries that contribute to a company's sales vary in importance. Therefore, one must calculate a common expression that will allow an equalized and weighted evaluation of important industries. This is a two-step process. First, calculate the "population" of those industries found to be important. Second, adjust these industry populations to reflect the percentage of business they generated.

Two ways of deriving the "population" of an industry in any geographic area are as follows:
1. Count the number of firms.
2. Count the number of employees.

Find the total population of important industries. Include only the "population" located in the areas where there is current sales coverage.

Example: Assume a firm receives 10% of its business from valve manufacturers (S.I.C. No. 3494). Second, assume this industry has a total population of 1,000 employees. Then the common expression for S.I.C. 3494 is that each employee is worth one-tenth of one percent of the company's business.

S.I.C. 3494 equals 10% of business.
S.I.C. 3494 total population = 1,000 employees.
Thus: $\dfrac{10\%}{1{,}000 \text{ Emp.}}$ = 1/10 of 1% or .01%.

What this says is that each employee in S.I.C. 3494 represents 1/10 of 1% of total company potential.

In the above example, it is possible to substitute the number of firms as the figure for the population. The choice of population should be guided by the common expression most representative of sales potential.

STEP THREE

Because a firm will want to evaluate each of its territories on an individual basis, step three of this analysis is designed to reveal the distribution of company potential on a geographic basis. The specific geographic areas to be included are current sales territories and all proposed territories.

The potential in a geographic area is the total of the "population" of that area's important customers multiplied by their respective common expressions. Specifically, one would list the total population in each significant industry group for each of his current and proposed sales territories. Then he would multiply each "population" by its common expression. Lastly, the results of the above multiplications would be totalled. Example for One Territory: Territory X:

S.I.C.	Population	x	Common Expression	=	Product
3,500	10,000		.0001%		1%
3,600	10,000		.0010%		10%
3,700	10,000		.0020%		20%
3,800	100		.0500%		5%
				TOTAL	36%

In the preceding example, Territory X contains 36% of the company's potential, divided between four industries as follows:
1. Industry 3500 1%
2. Industry 3600 10%

Marketing: the Management Way

   3. Industry 3700 20%
   4. Industry 3800 5%

Totalling the potential for each current territory will add up to 100%.

Example:

Assume the above company has four sales territories currently established: Territories W, X, Y, and Z. If the company was not planning to add any new territories, these four areas would contain 100% of the potential. Let us assume this 100% is distributed as follows:

   1. Territory W Contains 25%
   2. Territory X Contains 36%
   3. Territory Y Contains 25%
   4. Territory Z Contains 14%

When a company desires to calculate the potential of a proposed territory along with currently established areas, they must make an adjustment so that total company potential is not more than 100%.

Example: Assume that territories W, X, Y and Z have the same potentials as described in the previous example, but there is also a proposed territory (A) that has a calculated potential of 25%. By adding the potentials of A, W, X, Y and Z you would get a total company potential of 125%. Because it is not logical for a firm's territories to have more than 100% of the company's potential, it is necessary to derive a factor that will reduce the total potential of current and proposed territories back to 100%. This adjustment is made as follows:

   1. Divide the total potential of all established and proposed territories into 100%.

      Thus: $\dfrac{100\%}{125\%} = .8$

   2. Multiply the calculated potentials from each territory by the result of the above division.

The results in our hypothetical company would be as follows:

Territory	Calculated Potential	x	Adjusting Factor	=	Adjusted Potential
A	25%		.8		20.0%
W	25%		.8		20.0%
X	36%		.8		28.8%
Y	25%		.8		20.0%
Z	14%		.8		11.2%
TOTAL	125%				TOTAL 100%

182

STEP FOUR

A territory's performance is measured by comparing the amount of business it produced to the amount of business it should have produced. In our example, the four active territories should have divided the company's business as follows:

Territory W   25%
Territory X   36%
Territory Y   25%
Territory Z   14%

You will note that the above division is simply the territory's calculated potential. If these four territories did, in fact, divide the business as follows,

Territory W   25%
Territory X   20%
Territory Y   15%
Territory Z   40%,

individual territory performance would be calculated by dividing each calculated potential into the percentage of business that particular territory brought in.

Example:

Territory	Percentage of Sales	÷	Calculated Potential	=	Performance
W	25%		25%		100%
X	20%		36%		55%
Y	15%		25%		60%
Z	40%		14%		285%

In the situation just described, territory W would be considered average while territories X and Y would be considered below average. Territory Z would have to be considered above average.

If there are no unusual circumstances surrounding the territory calculated to have the highest performance, it is legitimate to set that territory's performance as the standard for all other territories. In our hypothetical example, the performance of territory Z would be set as a standard or benchmark. The performance of territories W, X and Y would then be recalculated as percentages of territory Z's performance.

Example:

Territory	Performance	Adjustment	Adjusted Performance
W	100%	100/285	35%
X	55%	55/285	19%
Y	60%	60/285	21%
Z	285%	285/785	100%

183

Once adjusted performance figures for each territory have been calculated, the percentages can be converted into dollars of sales expected when a territory performs up to par.

STEP FIVE

With its best territory identified (Territory Z), our hypothetical company can now calculate dollar sales potential on a company-wide and individual territory basis. Sales potential is defined as the dollar capability of a territory if its performance is equal to the performance of the best company.

To continue our example, let us assume that the four active territories brought in average annual sales of the following amounts over the past four years.

Territory W $25,000
Territory X $20,000
Territory Y $15,000
Territory Z $40,000

From Step Four we know that territory W's performance was only 35% of territory Z's and that territories X and Y had performances of 19% and 21% respectively. The total dollar potential for a territory is derived by dividing its average annual sales by its performance percentage.

Territory	Average Sales	÷	Percentage Performance	Average Sales Potential
W	$25,000		35%	$71,428
X	20,000		19%	105,263
Y	15,000		21%	71,428
Z	40,000		100%	40,000
	$100,000			$288,119

The above computation reveals the annual sales potential for each of the active sales territories over the past four years. It also tells that the company had unachieved sales of $188,119 per year. ($288,119 less $100,000).

As a final step in calculating total company sales potential, the potential sales of each prospective territory should be added into the total. In Step Three we calculated that the proposed territory (A) contained 20% of the total company potential. This means that the $288,119 potential of territories W, X, Y and Z is only 80% of the company's total potential of $359,547. ($288,119 ÷ .8 = $359,547). By a simple subtraction we find territory A has a potential of $71,428.

184

The following chart summarizes the information we now have available about our hypothetical company.

Territory	Avg. Sales	Sales Potential	Unachieved Sales
W	$25,000	$71,428	$46,428
X	20,000	105,263	85,263
Y	15,000	71,428	56,428
Z	40,000	40,000	0
A	0	71,428	71,428
	$100,000	$359,547	$259,547

It is now possible to answer the following questions.

QUESTION: What is a reasonable estimate of total sales potential?

ANSWER: $359,547 yearly.

QUESTION: What is a reasonable estimate of individual territory sales potential?

ANSWER: Territory W $71,428
Territory X $105,263
Territory Y $71,428
Territory Z $40,000
Territory A $71,428

QUESTION: What territories are getting the most mileage from available business?

ANSWER: Territory Z.

QUESTION: Which territories are lagging behind and are in need of special attention?

ANSWER: Territories W, X and Y. Evaluation of territory A must be put off for several years.

The sales potential figure we calculated in this example is not the same figure a marketing theoretican would have produced if you had asked him for a statement of sales or market potential. What we have produced is a highly workable estimate of what is reasonable for each sales territory to accomplish. It is this type of figure that is the basis for all market planning and evaluation. A reasonable estimate of sales expectations allows the further planning of sales territories and sales quotas and it also paves the way for meaningful sales analysis.

In our example, we calculated a performance percentage. As it stands, that figure is an interesting piece of academic information, but it must be pushed further to be useful. It must lead the way to answering the question of why one territory performs better than another. In the next section we will cover some of the available methods for determining the answer to our "Why" question.

185

Product, Customer and Cost Analysis

The three types of analysis we are going to look at are important for two reasons. First, they help diagnose why territories show low-performance percentages. Second, this type of analysis is a critical part of any control programme.

Product analysis starts by first defining what a product is. Is it each different catalogue number? Is it each product line? For sales analysis purposes, it is important to be able to call upon the most detailed breakdowns of product sale information. This does not mean you will always be using sales data for each catalogue item. It simply means that the record-keeping process should be able to produce detail when necessary.

In looking at product sales, the first thing a company might want to do is analyse the percentage of business coming from specific products. This type of analysis almost always produces surprises. The typical pattern in most multi-product firms is that 20% of the products produce 80-90% of the sales.

The next step in product analysis should lead the company to ask what products are sold to what customers. In the multi-product firm, gathering product data unrelated to customer type would become an academic exercise. For effective control and analysis, products must be related to customers.

As a third step, the company might look at sales of products by channels of distribution. When more than one sales channel is being used, product analysis by channel may provide insight into relative effectiveness.

Starting a new and much more simplified example, let us assume that Alpha Company sells three products: A, B and C. Territories have been established in such a way that each product should sell in a percentage equal to the territory's share of total potential.

Example: Territory X has 10% of company potential. It should therefore have 10% of the potential and sales of products A, B and C.

Company Sales:

Product A $100,000
Product B $50,000
Product C $25,000

Territory X Expected Sales:

A $100,000 x 10% = $10,000
B   50,000 x 10% = $5,000
C   25,000 x 10% = $2,500

186

Territory X Actual Sales:
Product A   1,000
Product B   5,000
Product C   500
Territory X Achievement by Product:
Product A $1,000 = 10%
            $\overline{10,000}$
Product B   5,000 = 100%
            $\overline{5,000}$
Product C   500 = 20%
            $\overline{2,500}$

If this type of analysis had followed the initial calculation of potential and penetration, we would know what areas of Territory X Needed Help:

We could make this type of analysis even more meaningful with a more realistic assumption on the distribution of product potential. If we return to our original example where Territory X was said to have 36% of company potential divided as follows:

S.I.C. 3500 =   1%
S.I.C. 3600 = 10%
S.I.C. 3700 = 20%
S.I.C. 3800 —   5%,

we should then calculate what % of each S.I.C. Nos. potential comes from each product.

Example: Product A accounts for 10% of company sales. By customer classification, the sales are divided as follows:
S.I.C. 3500 1%
S.I.C. 3600 3%
S.I.C. 3700 5%
S.I.C. 3800 1%

Territory X contains the following percentages of each S.I.C. numbers population:
S.I.C. 3500 10%
S.I.C. 3600 20%
S.I.C. 3700 10%
S.I.C. 3800 15%

By S.I.C. number and as a percentage of company potential, Territory X's sales of product A should be distributed as follows:
S.I.C. 3500 1% x 10% = .1%
S.I.C. 3600 3% x 20% = .6%

S.I.C. 3700 5% x 10% = .5%
S.I.C. 3800 1% x 50% = .5%

If Territory X's sales of product A as a percentage of total company sales are in fact as follows,

S.I.C. 3500 .1%
S.I.C. 3600 .3%
S.I.C. 3700 .2%
S.I.C. 3800 .1%

then we can get a measure of achievement for Territory X by customer for product A.

S.I.C.	% of Potential	% of Sales	Performance
3500	.1	.1	100%
3600	.6	.3	50%
3700	.5	.2	40%
3800	.5	.1	20%

Extending this example, one should calculate potential for each customer class by product for each of the company's territories. This would then allow you to take corrective action in the proper area. You could answer the question of which customers are purchasing products in adequate amounts in what territories.

A final analysis for Territory X might look as follows:

Territory X S.I.C. 3500 Product	% of Co. Potential	% of Actual Business	Performance %
A	.1	.1	100%
B	.5	1.9	380%
C	.3	2.0	666%
D	.1	1.0	1,000%
Total	1.00%	5.00%	500%

S.I.C. 3600 Product			
A	.6	.3	50%
B	5.4	1.7	32%
C	2.0	3.0	150%
D	2.0	.0	0%
Total	10.00%	5.00%	50%

188

S.I.C 3700
Product

A	.5	.2	40%
B	1.5	.8	53%
C	3.0	2.0	66%
D	5.0	2.0	40%
Total	20.00%	5.00%	25%

S.I.C, 3800
Product

A	.5	.1	20%
B	.5	.9	180%
C	2.0	1.0	50%
D	2.0	3.0	150%
Total	5.00%	5.00%	100%
Territory Total 36.00%		20.00%	55%

As a final step in the computational part of this exercise, one would have to convert the percentage figures into dollars. This procedure would follow the same steps as the conversion from percentage to dollars in our original example.

Once this type of analysis has been completed, a manager can begin to ask intelligent questions about sales performance. He knows which territories are performing up to par on each product and customer classification. But he does not yet have enough information to sit back and be satisfied for he knows nothing of the profits being lost or realized in each territory. We will come back to this point in a later section. Richard Crisp, in his book "Sales Planning and Control", summarizes the value of product type analysis very well.

"A recurring basic pattern in marketing, which is almost universally present in multiple-product companies, is one in which a given territory or district is strong on some products and weak on others. Product-type analysis permits you to identify and correct such a situation. A further value lies in the tendency for territories which are relatively strong on total performance to include a weakness in one or more major products. By identifying such situations, you can substitute constructive action for the tendency to coast, which sometimes develops in a territorial unit known to be strong."[3]

Perhaps the best way to summarize the value of product

3 Crisp, "Sales Planning and Control," McGraw-Hill, New York, 1961, p. 218.

analysis is to say that it points you in the right direction before you ask why someone is better or worse than someone else.

Customer Analysis

In our previous example on product analysis, we also included the beginnings of customer analysis. Customer analysis in its purest form is designed to highlight performance with respect to customer groups. In addition to there being important differences in the products purchased by different customer groups, there are likely to be vast differences in the way different customer groups are serviced.

Our discussion of product analysis showed that there are valid reasons for various customer groups having different purchasing patterns. One fact that was implicit in our product analysis example was that customer groups in the same industry with the same total population in different territories should be expected to have equal performance. This is very rarely the case. Because there is usually a wide difference of performance within customer groups between territories, we must carry out customer analysis to find out "why?".

It is a truism to say that without customer analysis, a firm has no way of knowing what customers are important and there is no way to know which territories are performing up to par within customer groups. There should be little doubt in your mind as to why customer analysis is important. Once important customers are identified and territory performances measured, effective control can come into existence.

The technicalities of customer analysis are very similar to those of product analysis. One simply calculates the company's average performance by customer group and then compares each territory to the average.

Customer analysis will help you answer the following questions:

1. Are there important geographical differences in customer concentration?
2. Has there been any shift or change in the relative and absolute importance of various customer groups?
3. Do territories vary significantly in their sales to the same customer groups?

We can summarize the value of customer-type analysis in the same way we summarized the value of product-type analysis. Customer analysis points you in the right direction before you ask why there are differences in performance amongst territories.

Cost Analysis

Sales territory, product-type and customer analysis can all remain in the category of academic exercises if one does not incorporate some type of cost and profit analysis. Sales contribution to margin ratios must be calculated so that the weak and strong links in each territory can be analysed. Cost analysis can be used to pinpoint the performance of individual salesmen and sales offices.

If the accounting data is available, a total contribution to margin figure should be calculated for each salesman. A ratio should then be calculated between sales and contribution to margin. A company average should be established and each salesman compared to the company average. The same thing should be done for each sales territory.

When cost and sales data is available in great detail, the sales analysis team should be calculating contribution to margin for customer types and for product types.

With adequate cost data, a firm could answer each of the following questions:

1. Are those territories that are performing well on product and customer analysis also performing well from a profit standpoint?
2. Within each territory, are these salesmen concentrating on the sales of low margin, easy to sell items?
3. Which are the sales territories and who are the salesmen that are producing the most contribution to margin in absolute terms and with respect to sales and sales potential?

Without going through the mechanics, it is quite conceivable that territory customer and product potential could be expressed in terms of contribution to margin. If you remember our original example of sales analysis, we used total sales as the base for calculating a common expression with which to measure potential. If one used a contribution to margin figure, his product, customer and territory analysis would automatically include the necessary profit orientation.

Territory Boundaries and Number of Salesmen

Our discussion of territory boundaries will begin with the asking and answering of a question. Why does a firm establish sales territory boundaries? When all peripheral answers are eliminated, the central reason of providing a means to control

191

and evaluate marketing activity emerges. If control and evaluation are the important reasons for setting up territories, it stands to reason there should be a direct relationship between control and evaluation devices and sales territory establishment.

One may not see the immediate relationship between territory boundaries and number of salesmen. The relationship will become clear when we think of the territory as the framework through which you can determine if you have adequate sales coverage. Through sales analysis, which invariably requires territory analysis, it is possible to identify those areas where more or less sales coverage is needed, and this, in effect, answers the question of how many salesmen are necessary.

Let us now return to the relationship between territories and control or evaluation. In the ideal situation, we would like our territories to all be of equal size in terms of potential and salesman's work load. This would then make the job of comparisons very easy. We would also like the territory to be a relatively small unit so that one territory will not have both good and bad coverage within its boundaries.

Before getting into the actual problems of setting up territories, let us look at some of the practical problems involved. If the territory is to serve as a control and evaluation unit, you must be able to collect information about the potential within its border. In most cases, information about particular populations is made available by government authorities and the information is related to political boundaries, such as cities, states and other governmental areas. There is no necessary logic between the factors that govern political boundaries and the factors that should determine territory boundaries. Therefore, the blind acceptance of a city or any other governmental area as a territory boundary must be questioned. If you choose any other boundaries than the political type, you may not be able to get population data at a reasonable cost.

There are two basic methods for deciding where or how to set sales territory boundaries and how many salesmen are needed for each territory. Our examples will be over-simplified but adequate to demonstrate the principles involved. For want of better names, we will call the two methods the Build Up and Break Down methods.

In the Build Up method, one determines the number, location and size of customers. We then determine what is the best call pattern to cover the accounts. Next, the necessary salesmen

192

are assigned to sell these accounts, and finally, groups of salesmen are joined into logical control groups.

The Break Down method works as follows:

1. Determine total company potential.
2. Determine sales volume expected from each salesman.
3. Determine the number of salesmen needed.
4. Establish territories.

Both the Build Up and Break Down methods depend on the company having large amounts of data available. In the Build Up method you must have complete lists of all potential customers and where they are located. This means the company must first know who the customer is and then locate him. Determining who, in general terms, is your customer can come from past sales records. Identifying specific companies and/or people along with their location is sometimes quite difficult.

Assuming you can locate customers, the Build Up method says you must then determine a desirable call pattern. Call patterns are determined by how many calls a person can make in a day and how many times a company must be called on in a specific time period. If a company has done no previous sales analysis, it would be most difficult to set up a call pattern. If, on the other hand, the management has perfomed sales analysis, it can look to its better performing territories' salesmen and customer groups to find out what call pattern is currently being used.

One must then assign accounts to salesmen and then group salesmen into control units or territories. The only guidance we can give in a general sense is that you want to keep all territories as similar as possible and as small as possible without forfeiting managerial and sales efficiency.

The Break Down method of establishing a territory starts off with the assumption that the company knows its total sales potential. If the company has done sales analysis, there is a good chance that it does have a reasonable estimate of this figure. As a second step, the Break Down method requires a sales estimate figure for each salesman. Again, this information can be gained from a good sales analysis. This information can be broken down by customer and product from a good sales analysis. The final steps of the Break Down method are similar to the Build Up method. You determine how many salesmen are needed and where they are needed and then you build reasonable control units.

One cannot depend entirely on a mathematical model to tell him how to set up a territory or how many salesmen are necessary. There are many qualitative considerations that must be made. Some of these considerations are:

1. Variation in the nature of the job to be done.
2. Variation in products being sold.
3. Channel of distribution in area.
4. Stage of market development in the area.
5. Competition in the area.
6. Ethnic factors.
7. Transportation facilities.
8. Topography and climate.[4]

Conclusion

Our hope in presenting this somewhat detailed example of sales analysis and its problems was to show that there is a rational and logical way to control and evaluate the sales force. We do not suggest that there is any one way to go about evaluation and control. The only thing we do suggest is that the sales force can be controlled and evaluated if one is willing to make the effort.

[4] Stanton & Buskirk, *Management of the Sales Force,* Richard D. Irwin Inc., Homewood, Illinois, Rev. Ed., 1964, pp. 609-612.

DISCUSSION QUESTIONS

1. How has the sales management job changed in companies that have accepted a customer orientation?
2. Discuss the benefit to be derived from various types of sales analysis.
3. What factors should govern the establishment of sales territories?
4. Discuss the importance of control in the sales management job.
5. What information is necessary to do an effective job of sales management?

BIBLIOGRAPHY

ALDERSON & GREEN: *Planning and Problem Solving in Marketing*, Richard D. Irwin Inc., Homewood, Ill., U.S.A.

CRISP: *Sales Planning and Control*, McGraw-Hill, New York, N.Y., U.S.A.

STANTON & BUSKIRK: *Management of the Sales Force*, Richard D. Irwin Inc., Homewood, Ill., U.S.A.

11

Control of the
Marketing Effort

By its very nature, marketing cries out for effective control. This same nature makes control of the marketing effort a most difficult job. The marketing manager's control job is made difficult because his department's performance is influenced by a large number of uncontrollable factors. Marketing is also the victim of quick and often unpredictable change.

This discussion will take a close look at the nature of control and what a marketing manager can hope to achieve through a control system. An attempt will be made to design a control system that will have general marketing application. It is through control that the marketing effort is tied together. It is through our discussion of control that we hope to bring together our entire discussion of marketing.

The Nature of Control

Change, the cause of all management problems, creates the need for control. As a business system's susceptibility to change increases, the system's need for control also increases. Marketing systems are vulnerable to change in so many ways that the need for control is obvious. "The procedure of monitoring changes in the environment for the purpose of detecting significant differences between expected and actual results so as to make appropriate adjustments" is a suitable working definition of control.

For control to exist, two criteria must be met. Control parameters must not be so wide as to create a system that is called "in control" under all circumstances. Secondly, the decisions

196

available to the controller must allow him to do something about an "out of control" system. While these criteria seem obvious, all too many control systems violate one or the other rule.

Marketing management's area of control is centred in the marketing mix. It can act in the areas of product planning, pricing, branding, channels of distribution, personal selling, advertising, special promotions, packaging, servicing, physical handling and fact finding. In each of these areas, management has the ability to make controlling decisions.

The interrelationships of all elements in the marketing mix are continuous and dynamic. Yet, the marketing manager must be able to factor out the single item in the mix that is out of control. All too often, this type of factoring is impossible. The first warning a marketing manager may get that a system is out of control is when the accountant tells him profits have dropped below acceptable standards. On other occasions, it may be a market research group that tells him he has lost another twenty percent of the market. Controlling from historic data has some chance to be effective in certain, very stable industries. In more dynamic industries, other alternatives are needed.

Automatic process control has taught us a great deal. A prime lesson has been that it is often cheaper to install a monitoring device that will warn of a change in a system before it happens, rather than waiting for the change to take place and then correcting the situation. Sophisticated control systems monitor for expectant change and set up corrective action before a change can take place.

A household example of this type of system is an advanced action thermostat. In this system, there is an outdoor thermometer which triggers the indoor thermostat under conditions of extreme temperature change. The heating or air conditioning system can then start to compensate for the expected change in household temperature before the change occurs.

In the marketing situation, we cannot point to many examples of continuous monitoring and self-correcting control systems. Inventory control systems are now available in a form that allows automatic calculation of usage, forecasting of future usage, ordering of material and optimal usage of available inventory. Specific areas of marketing management, such as pricing, advertising, packaging, channel management and sales, are still a long way from automatic control. It is hoped that this discussion will speed up the introduction of future control systems.

Purpose of Control

Traditional thinking about control and control systems in management has been rather mundane. We often hear people justify the existence of a control system on the basis of it being a device to enable you to stop mistakes. Others say control systems permit you to salvage a system before it goes under. Still others say control systems are needed so that you can fix blame on guilty people and provide incentive for better management. Finally, there is a group that sees control as a means of preventing the re-occurrence of old mistakes.

The above are all qualities of a control system, but stopping mistakes, salvage, blame, incentives and preventing re-occurrence of mistakes should not be the motivation behind a control system. The purpose of a control system must be stated in much broader terms. Control systems are planning and integrating devices. It is a control system that should unite an entire organization towards one goal. It is the framework for all organization planning.

> "Marketing control is both a process and a concept. It is part of the process of management, and in systems terms indivisible from planning and organization. Control is also a continuous and pervasive process of establishing standards, measurement of performance, comparison, evaluation, and adjustment of marketing policies, programmes and procedures. The modern concept of marketing control is that it consists of more than the measurement and audit function. It is both diagnostic and prognostic. Control is partly utilized to secure the most efficient use of financial, human, and physical resources consistent with objectives. . . . Effective control requires integrated management skills in planning and goal setting, establishing performance standards, comparing results against standards. . . . The customer is the ultimate controller of marketing and firm operations, and so controls many corporate programmes and holds veto power over all marketing programmes. . . ."[1]

Looked at in this way, control becomes much more than its traditional image. It is from this newer and more meaningful viewpoint that we will discuss control of the marketing effort.

The Control System

The first requirement for any control system is something to control. From the firm's viewpoint, this "controlled system" is

---

[1] Kelly, Marketing Strategy & Functions, Prentice-Hall, N.J., 1965, p. 23.

the environment or, in a smaller sense, the market place. It is the environment that corporate effort is attempting to control. The marketing department attempts to guide consumer choice and thereby control consumer behaviour. By giving the environment the name, "controlled system", we are not negating nor is it meant to infer that the environment does not control the effort to a very large extent.

In control system terminology, each individual marketing programme becomes a "control element". Control "elements" are the devices by which we hope to control the "controlled system". A control element might be the establishment of a sales territory or the running of a particular advertisement. Each control element has a specific function and is responsible for a particular effect on the "controlled system".

From our earlier discussion, you will remember that we said control depends on having parameters defining "in" and "out" of control systems. To this, we must add that control depends on having a device that will measure the status of the "controlled system" so that we can compare this status to our parameters. In control system terminology, this means there must be a "sensing system" and a "comparitor". The "sensing system" most often installed for marketing purposes is the marketing research department. Locating the "comparitor" is a somewhat more difficult task. Theoretically, the comparitor should be the part of the organization that has the responsibility for setting the goals of the marketing department. In reality, the "comparitor" is often a person charged with the responsibility of maintaining only one part of the marketing department. We have given this person the name "sub-comparitor". The sub-comparitor's position might be of the product manager type or advertising manager type, depending on the organization.

Each functional department in a properly controlled organization will exist within a specific control system. In turn, it will be related to corporate and/or divisional objectives through a unifying control system called a "level one" control system. The "level one" control system would become active when the functional or "level two" control system could not cope with a situation.

Figure Six shows a marketing control system in diagrammatic form. The remainder of our discussion will attempt to outline how a control system might work in operation. We will look at such things as how the control system provides for establishment of goals, how targets are established along with parametric controls for the target. We will be most interested in

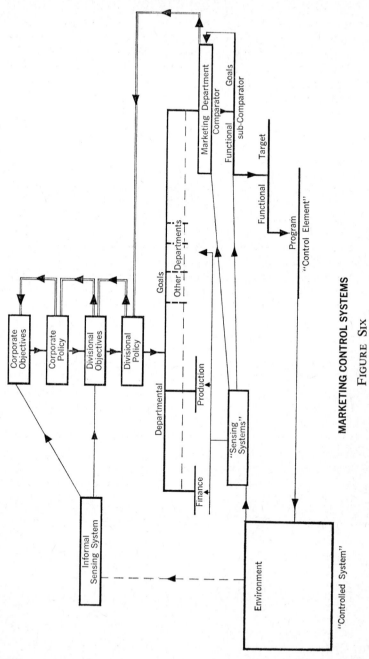

MARKETING CONTROL SYSTEMS

FIGURE SIX

showing how those items which influence a target and the targets themselves can be turned into control systems.

Early in our discussion we said the ideal type of control system would be one that gave a warning before the system went out of control. For this type of warning system to exist in marketing, it means that each goal and target must be set with an understanding of the factors that will determine success or failure. Knowing that market share has dropped from 25% to 23% provides an after-the-event type of control. What is desired is a set of "comparators" that react as a warning system when a goal is not going to be reached.

In business, we do not want to be changing programmes and goals every time there is the slightest hint of trouble. What we want is a multi-level warning system. Perhaps a three-level system much like a quality control system, where measurements above one, two and three standard deviations exist, is appropriate for marketing systems. The first level warning requires no action other than the making of an impression. A second-level warning would start investigation into cause and the possible implementation of corrective measures. When a third-level warning is received, it would require immediate attention.

Control and Planning

In our earliest discussion of planning we outlined the planning job as a five-stage process running from "establishing objectives" to "selecting a course of action". We also mentioned that control was an essential part of planning, but we did not discuss control in any detail. If we were to follow our original outline of planning, we would put in a step 6—"designing the control system". Let us now take a closer look at the relationship between planning and control.

Our formal definition of control contained the following outline of steps involved:

1. Monitoring change.
2. Detecting significant differences between expected and actual results.
3. Making appropriate adjustments.

It is the third step, "making appropriate adjustments", that ties a control system into planning. There will be many instances when a minor adjustment cannot bring an "out of control" system back into control. In these circumstances and in the case where your early warning system tells you of an impending major change, making the appropriate change re-

201

quires a repeat of the entire planning process. Depending on the particular plan that has gone, or is about to go out of control, replanning may involve changing a programme, functional target, functional goal, departmental goal, or divisional and/or corporate objectives and policy.

The actual time when control and plan are tied together is when one is working out the administrative detail of the particular plan. According to Alderson and Green, this process contains the following six steps:

"(a) Manual of instructions stating individual responsibilities under plan.
(b) Standards of performance to measure success of plan such as sales forecasts or budget variances.
(c) Rules of action for handling exceptions.
(d) Situations to be referred to superiors for decision.
(e) Bonus compensation or other incentive for performance under plan.
(f) Specified reports for control while operation is in progress."[2]

If we assume that some type of guided growth is a basic corporate objective, we must not design a control system that will inhibit growth. Making the corporate objective and all of its lower level goals, targets and programmes part of the control system prevents the control system from negating an objective. Control systems, like most other systems of behaviour, will attempt to find the easiest path to equilibrium. Unless each part of the control system is related to a specific objective, there is a possibility of the lower portions of the corporate structure reaching some sort of control equilibrium without satisfying the total corporate objective.

By placing the objectives, goals, targets and programmes of a corporation into the control system, we ensure that these four statements or desires are expressed in a form that allows control. If the person designing some portion of a marketing plan realizes that he must also design an appropriate control system, he forces himself to take a sound, logical approach. He is much more apt to thoroughly study the factors that can affect his plan. He will seek to quantify the relationship between these various factors.

Control of the Marketing Mix

Control of the many parts of the marketing mix depends on the meeting of certain requirements. First, we must be able

---

[2] Green, op. cit., p. 635.

to define a standard of performance for each element in the mix. The development of a standard will depend on the statement of an objective. Measuring performance and determining if a standard or objective has been met will depend on a measuring device being available. Finally, the availability of a measuring device will depend very much on the understanding one has of the factor being measured. In this concluding section we will look at the objectives, standards of performance, measuring devices and influencing factors within the various parts of the marketing mix.

Product Planning

For the sake of uniformity of coverage, we will begin this part of our discussion with an analysis of the product planning control system. You will remember that product planning was the first part of the marketing mix we looked at in any great detail. What are the objectives of product planning? How might these objectives be stated so as to aid in the control of product planning?

When pressed for a statement of product development objectives, management will usually offer some financial objective. "Many facets of company objectives may provide the motivation behind product development. Some examples, FINANCIAL GROWTH (Greater Net Profit) . . . FINANCIAL EFFICIENCY (Greater return on assets or equity) . . . FINANCIAL STABILITY (Small range of earnings fluctuation over time) . . . FINANCIAL CERTAINTY (probability of actual earnings equalling predicted earnings) . . . FINANCIAL DURABILITY (Years of earnings flows) . . ."[3]

One very rarely gets a statement of the personal motivations behind new product development. Non-financial objectives, such as prestige, may be of equal importance to the financial objective, but it is not usually mentioned as a reason for product development.

Without carrying the discussion very far, it is easy to see that a generalized statement of financial and personal objectives would not lead to an acceptable control system. In a properly oriented marketing company, the objectives of product planning must start with some consideration of consumer needs to be fulfilled. Perhaps a statement of objectives that included consideration of consumer needs, financial objectives and

---

3 Stewart, "Product Development" in *Science in Marketing,* Ed. Schwartz, Wiley & Sons Inc., New York, 1965, pp. 164-165.

personal objectives would lead to a workable and controlled system of product development. These statements must be definite enough to guide the actions of subordinates but not so specific as to prohibit initiative.

With a semi-specific set of objectives or goals to direct its activities, the product development group must develop a detailed set of operational objectives or targets. The successful completion of each of these targets should lead to the satisfaction of the departmental goal. This means that there should be targets or performance standards set for exploration, screening, business analysis, development, testing and commercialization. What we are saying is that controls should be established in conformance with the needs of each stage in the product evolution cycle.

Ralph W. Jones deals with the problem of control of product planning in an article called "Management of New Products". He outlines the control requirements of product development as follows:

"7. New idea creation can be directed and controlled to achieve improved pertinence and quality of product ideas. . . .

8. New product selection is accomplished by a continuing series of evaluation in all stages, no single screening is adequate. . . .

9. Selection standards for products to be developed should be upgraded persistently to achieve an ever-increasing yield from available manpower on resources.

10. Product planning requires . . . development of specifications and a programme for each product prior to laboratory project. . . .

11. The more concisely corporate objectives are stated, the more chance there will be retaining the best ideas and only rejecting the poor ideas."[4]

The types of controls and standards that Jones is talking about are of the more common after-the-event type. If one could develop warning system controls for product development, the after-event type of control would become less critical. There would be no benefit in our outlining a proposed warning system for a hypothetical product development project. Each project or company will need its own specific controls. The best we can do at this stage is to review the internal and external factors that will influence the success of product development.

Some very basic considerations that will affect the future success of a product are financial investment, channels of dis-

---

4 Jones, "Management of New Products," *Journal of Industrial Engineering,* Vol. IX, No. 5 (Sept./Oct., 1958), pp. 434-5.

204

tribution, effect on old products, effect on competition, cyclical stability, raw materials, effect on manufacturing load, effect on marketing mix and effect on organization. Inventorying of corporate resources, such as financial strength, physical plant, raw materials, personnel, special experience, management and reputation, should all be built into an early warning system. All possible social and economic changes should be under constant observation. Finally, a continuous evaluation of the consumer and his wants is a necessary part of any control system.

Identifying the interdepartmental ramifications of product development and identifying the effect of product development on the parts of the marketing mix can be an extraordinarily difficult job. Hopefully, the interdepartmental and systems type of approach suggested by this author will make the job tolerable, if not easy.

Pricing

What is the objective of a pricing decision? If we can answer this question, we can develop a control system for the pricing function. The economist does not have any difficulty in explaining the objectives of a price within the macro-economic environment. Price is visualized as the prime mover in clearing the market. For the businessman, the problem is not quite as simple. He knows that it will take more than the "right" price to move his production. If price is not to act as the prime mover, we must then learn to define the objective of any price or price decision.

At this stage, it should no longer be necessary to repeat that the functional goals of price, when satisfied, should lead to the satisfaction of marketing goals and then corporate objectives. Determining the objectives for any pricing decision starts by deciding how prices are to be used in the overall marketing strategy. Some of the most frequently stated objectives of a price decision are:

"1. Attainment of a target rate of return. Prices are set so that they will yield some designated return on investment. . . .

2. To maintain or improve the company's share of the market. . . .

3. Stabilisation of price and margin. . . .

4. Pricing to meet or follow competition. . . ."[5]

---

[5] Backman, "Pricing," in Schwartz, op. cit., p. 254.

We must now ask ourselves if these objectives are adequate for developing a control system. It seems that this group of objectives is too general to provide the type of guidance necessary to establish a control system.

In developing operational targets for a price decision, one must first fully describe the part price is going to play in the marketing mix. The individual responsible for making final decisions about pricing programmes must know what part pricing is going to play in the total marketing effort. Price can be either an active or passive partner in the marketing mix. Prices can be essentially stable or allowed to fluctuate freely in response to market conditions. Retail prices can be controlled by the manufacturer or the manufacturer can relinquish control to other segments of the trade channel.

It would seem that pricing goals or objectives should also be stated in relation to their effect on demand and profit. Stating that a price should return a specific rate of return may lead to sub-optimization of corporate objectives. Prices must be set so that they are consistent with the market target of the company or division. Price programmes must be in tune with the brand image that is desired by the company. Pricing objectives should be stated so that they explain their part in achieving the marketing objective.

While broad and generalized objectives may give the price-setter enough guidance to set prices that are consistent with marketing objectives, he does not have enough to develop a control system. Targets of a predictive nature must be developed. The pricer must learn what factors govern the effectiveness of his price and what factors work to change this effectiveness.

If the pricer understands the influence of all parties interested in his price, he stands a good chance of measuring the impact of his decisions. In other words, the influence of customers, competition, general economic factors, government, suppliers, resellers and other corporate departments must be analysed. A good deal of this type of information can be approximated by analysing past history. If past history shows any pattern at all, the price-setter can develop measurements of effectiveness that will serve as a warning system.

The pricer will be looking to each of the factors that influence the effectiveness of a pricing decision for hints or evidence of adverse reaction. He will be looking for indicators that might suggest that changes in a price or price policy would be advantageous. Anticipating troubles and preparing contingency plans for the pricing decision will add to pricing management the extra measure of control necessary for effective management in all segments of the marketing mix.

Most traditional marketing literature relates price to sales as a measure of pricing effectiveness; because the ultimate sales of any product are the result of many interacting forces, it is not reasonable to say that adequate or inadequate sales are the result of a price decision. In fact, if management realizes that price is only one contributing factor in a product's success, it will be easier to develop a system of control that does measure pricing effectiveness.

Channels of Distribution

In our first discussion of channels of distribution, we emphasized the fact that channels could be managed. The purpose of this section is to show how management can develop a control system for its channel(s) of distribution. David Revzan lists six factors or criteria that are the basis for evaluating channel effectiveness. The presumption is that if one can determine the six pieces of information Revzan requires, he can manage his trade channel.

"(1) To determine the contribution of channel alternatives to the achievement of the company's over-all marketing programme, in quantitative and qualitative units;
"(2) to determine, more specifically, the direct and indirect relationship between channel alternatives and the degree of market penetration of the company's product lines, area by area;
"(3) to determine the contribution of channel alternatives to customer recognition and acceptance of the company's sales promotional campaigns;
"(4) to determine the contribution of the channel to the company's complete knowledge of the characteristics of the market it services;
"(5) to determine the contribution of the channel to the company's favourable or unfavourable cost-profit position, product line by product line, and market area by market area; and
"(6) to determine the contribution of each channel alternative to the degree of aggressiveness of the company's marketing programme."[6]

From the viewpoint of developing a control system, the Revzan criteria are a good starting point. If we turn these criteria around just slightly, we see that Revzan has implied that the company knows what part the channel plays in con-

[6] Revzan, *Wholesaling in Marketing Organizations*, Wiley & Sons, New York, 1961, p. 151.

tributing to the success of the marketing programme. Once the company knows what effect the channel has on the achievement of the over-all marketing programme, the degree of market penetration, customer recognition, knowledge of customer needs, cost-profit relationships and the aggressiveness of the company marketing programme, it should find out why these relationships exist.

If satisfactory performance in each of the Revzan criteria means the channel is working correctly, then the manager will want to have a warning system that tells him when the system is going to go out of control. For example, the manager will want to know how the channel affects his cost-profit position. He will want complete details of how costs and profits are generated within the channel. With this information he can then set control limits on each of the cost-profit generators. These limits, when exceeded, will be the warning that the cost-profit relationship is apt to go out of control. The manager still has time to take corrective action when he watches the channel in this way. He should never be faced with the situation that his channel is collapsing around him and he doesn't know it is happening.

To summarize the requirements of a channel control system we see the following factors as being necessary:

1. A statement of the part the channel is to play in achieving the marketing objective.
2. Complete understanding of how the channel contributes to the achievement of a marketing objective.
3. Control specifications for all factors within the channel of distribution that contribute to the achievement of a marketing objective.

Promotion: Personal and Non-Personal

There is a definite reason for grouping a discussion of personal and non-personal promotional control systems. Personal and non-personal promotional activities must be thought of as complementary devices. Changing any single item of promotion has an immediate response and effect on all other promotional activities. There is no reason for advertising and personal selling to be in competition for a larger slice of the budget. The two devices should be searching for their optimal balance point.

The objectives of all promotional activities are intimately inter-related. Controlling promotional activity starts in the same way as controlling all other parts of the marketing mix. First,

208

the specific objective to be achieved by advertising, personal selling, sales promotion and publicity must be decided. You could even include the promotional objectives of package design in this problem. The objectives of each item in the promotional mix must be set with a realization of how they are inter-related.

Setting of any objective really assumes an understanding of the process of achieving that objective. In setting the promotional objectives for his firm, the manager must know how to achieve these objectives and what factors will affect or determine the success of his effort. When the manager knows how each element of the environment affects his successful completion of a promotional campaign, he can translate his objectives into a programme. This programme, when broken down into its smallest parts, becomes the promotional control system. Successfully bringing each affecting factor into the proper state of nature will mean the automatic achievement of the promotional objective.

If we assume that one set of advertising objectives is the creation of certain psychological states of mind, we might say that one type of advertising control system would be the following: the creation of X amount of "initial attention, perception, continued favourable attention or interest, comprehension, feeling, emotion, motivation, belief, intentions, decisions, imagery, association, recall and recognition."[7] To find out if his advertising objective is being achieved, the manager must then develop a sensing system that will relate a true measurement of the above factors.

Looking at the opposite side of the promotional picture, we often hear the sales manager state his objective as some particular level of sales. As a control device, "sales" leave much to be desired. Even "sales" with some statement of profitability leaves much to be desired. Sales, goals or objectives should be used to determine the operational goals of the sales department. In other words, the sales job must be broken down into its actual step-by-step procedure and a control measurement set up at each level.

Control of the sales effort assumes that one knows the procedure that will be most effective in producing profitable sales or sales that meet the marketing objective. The sales manager or the marketing manager of an industrial equipment company might know that his salesman will be most effective when

---

[7] Britt and Lucas, *Measuring Advertising Effectiveness*, McGraw-Hill, New York, 1963, p. 116.

dealing with plant managers instead of purchasing agents; he may know that his equipment is sold best when a trial is accepted; he may know that certain customers require one call pattern and others a different call pattern. These particular sales tools or sales programmes should be built into the control system. This type of control will allow intelligent decisions to be made. Controlling from sales figures alone is at best a dangerous undertaking.

Sales management has one very effective control system at its disposal. National, divisional, territory and individual sales figures are all compiled from the item by item records generated by individual sales. This single fact gives the sales manager an ability to pinpoint weakness and deficiency in a way that is not available to many other managers. When sales potential in a territory or for an individual salesman is not being achieved, the sales manager's control system should quickly point out why this is happening.

Control and Expected Value

If the marketing control problem is reduced to a quantitative decision, it can be stated that control has as its purpose the maximization of expected value. Looking at the control problem as an exercise in quantitative decision-making is a logical extension of the planning-control sequence.

The objectives and/or targets of any programme become the payoffs that one hopes to maximize. Without a control system to measure the difficulty of achieving and the progress being made towards achieving a target, decision-making remains in the category of decision-making under conditions of uncertainty. Once a control system comes into existence, it is possible to change decision-making from an essentially intuitive art to a process of logical and rational semi-science. A control system that is working correctly will tell you the probability of a particular event and it will tell you when that probability is changing.

Knowing the probability of an event and being able to watch how that probability is changing allows you to calculate the expected value of a decision. In addition to being able to calculate expected value, you can also calculate how much to spend on changing the probability or bringing the system into tighter control.

If the stimulation of a re-planning cycle is one of the objectives of a control system, reducing the control problem to one of a quantitative decision is an invaluable aid. One of the steps in any complete quantitative decision process is the statement of all the possible alternatives. When a control system flashes that a system may be going out of control or has gone out of control, one could be required to re-study all possible alternatives and re-evaluate those alternatives to find the decision that maximizes expected payoff.

Control Systems and Budgeting

One purpose in developing a control system is to achieve an optimal distribution of the corporation's scarce resources. The physical device an organization uses in keeping track of the allocation of its resources and the device it uses in matching expected results against actual results is very often called the budget. In the concept of control that has been developed throughout this book, the budget can be looked on as the central control tool. All objectives, policies, goals, targets and standards must be matched against resource availability. Allocation of available resources must be made with reference to the expected value of each unit of resource utilized.

While budgets are most often thought of as financial control devices, there is no reason to limit their use to purely financial problems. If a company has non-financial objectives, a budgeting process must be established that can relate resource output to the particular type of non-financial return desired.

The budget in effect is the total corporate plan with all its possible ramifications. It is the budget that changes an idea into a business proposition.

In much the same way that corporate objectives finally develop into programme targets, the corporate budget will develop into a programme budget. With a series of budgets as the physical evidence of all plans and their expected payoffs, it becomes possible to set up a monitoring system that can tie all the budgets together.

Control and the Computer

To achieve the type of control one would like in a large corporation requires some type of automated information processing. The sheer physical task of keeping track of all system inputs and outputs makes manual-human control of a system

211

impossible. Even if we could find a group of super-humans that could keep track of all system inputs and outputs, it is unlikely that this group of people would ever finish the mathematical computations necessary to relate changes in input and output.

The modern computer can be used as a repository for all input-output data available to the corporation. It can be programmed to monitor systems and warn when they are about to go out of control. The computer can, if properly programmed, relate the effects of most important events taking place within and outside of the company.

If there were no restrictions on the capacity of a computer, and a company had an infinite supply of money and the company knew what information was necessary and it had the ability to collect this information, then a computer could theoretically be programmed to make all decisions necessary to run the company.

Leaving the world of "Oz" and coming back to reality, we don't have to be afraid of being displaced by computers. All computers to date have limitations on their capacity. No firm has unlimited financial resources. There is so much that we do not know about the working of the market place that we could never know all the information necessary to make a decision. And finally, we have not developed an information collecting system capable of gathering all of the limited amount of data we now require.

Perhaps the greatest benefit of using a computer as the information processing unit in a control system is that it requires planning and control decisions to be logical. A computer will not follow an illogical set of instructions. The computer will tell us every time we make a decision that seems to contradict the logically valid decision. The computer will also warn of any possible sub-optimization of corporate objectives.

Because of its ability to analyse an event as it is taking place, the computer makes it possible to re-plan before a system is out of control. If a control system had to wait for the time lapse involved in the human transmission of information, it is highly improbable that a system could be corrected before a serious mishap took place.

We must now address ourselves to the problem of deciding which control systems get put on to a computer and how much we spend on collecting the information necessary for the control system to work. The second part of this problem is the easier to answer. Going back to our earlier discussion of quantitative decision-making, we showed how to make the decision of whether or not to purchase market information. It was shown that one could calculate the increase in expected value of an alternative when new information became available. The cost of the information was compared to the increase in expected value. If the cost of the information was lower than the increase in expected value, then it paid to collect the information.

Deciding which control systems should be put into a computer of limited capacity or in a firm where there are restrictions on financial capacity should follow the same reasoning as the decision to purchase market data. In other words, one would calculate the increase in payoff generated in putting alternative control systems onto the computer. Those that generated the largest increases in payoff would be the first candidates for computerization.

Analysing the utilization of computer capacity in this way will prevent the computer being used only as a replacement for clerical help. While a computer is highly suited to doing the task of many clerks, it can also solve high-level management problems. Reducing the risk of probability of being wrong on major marketing programmes, capital budgeting decisions and machine and labour allocation *may be* much more profitable than replacing one hundred clerks. The words *may be* were used for a specific purpose in the preceding sentence. There will be occasions when the reduction of clerical help is the most profitable function a computer can be put to.

Conclusion

Control requirements, much like all other parts of marketing management, will vary from company to company. The purpose of this chapter has been to introduce a concept of control that will lead to more effective management. Control must be visualized as the management function that unites the entire corporation. Hopefully this discussion of control has also united the many pages that have passed betwen the beginning and the end of this book.

DISCUSSION QUESTIONS

1. What is control and what is the control function in marketing?
2. How is control related to marketing planning?
3. Describe a generalized control system for a marketing department.
4. What requirements does a control system place on the determination of the marketing mix?
5. What part does the computer serve in marketing control systems?

BIBLIOGRAPHY

ALDERSON & SHAPIRO (Ed.): *Marketing and the Computer*, Prentice-Hall, N.J., U.S.A., 1963.

COX, ALDERSON & SHAPIRO: *Theory in Marketing*, 1st and 2nd Series, Richard D. Irwin Inc., Homewood, Ill., U.S.A.

FRANK, KUEHN & MASSEY: *Quantitative Techniques in Marketing*, Richard D. Irwin Inc., Homewood, Ill., U.S.A., 1962.

KELLY: *Marketing Strategy and Functions*, Prentice-Hall, N.J., U.S.A., 1965.

SCHWARTZ (Ed.): *Science in Marketing*, Wiley and Sons Inc., New York, N.Y., 1965.

Index

Marketing: the Management Way

Control—*continued*
promotion, 208
purpose, 198
self regulating, 197
systems, 198
Control and Planning, 201
Costs, 102
book, 104
common, 104
direct, 104
fixed, 103
future, 103
historical, 104
incremental, 104
indirect, 104
long run, 103
marginal, 104
opportunity, 103
outlay, 103
out of pocket, 104
past, 103
replacement, 104
short run, 103
traceable, 104
variable, 103
Cost Analysis, 186, 191
Cues, 31
Culture, 25
Customer Analysis, 186, 190
Customer Orientation, 3

Defence, 27
Decision Criteria, 54
average, 54
expected payoff, 55
maximum, 54
minimax, 54
Depth Interview, 41
Differential Advantage, 18-19
Discontinuous Change, 50, 64
Discounts, 108
cash, 109
functional, 109
geographic, 109
negotiated, 110
quantity, 109
timing, 110

Distribution Problems, 137
Drucker, Peter, 45

Economic Models, 14-17
Exploitation, 27

Facilities, 52
Family, 29
Family Life Cycle, 29
Family Structure, 30
Forecasting,
exponential smoothing, 65
short run, 64
trend extrapolation, 64
Forecasts, 61
barometric, 61, 62
econometric, 61, 63
naive, 61, 62
opinion polling, 61, 63

Gatekeeper, 28
Group Behaviour, 27

Heterogeneous Markets, 17, 18

Imperfect Competition, 14, 15
Incremental Profits, 81
Information, 66
external, 67
internal, 67
primary, 66
secondary, 66
sources, 68
validity, 67
Innovation
management, 6, 7
Innovators, 31
Instrumental Behaviour, 30
Interaction, 26

Learning, 27, 30
Long Range Planning, 45, 46

Management
negotiative process, 8
Manufacturers' Agents, 136
Marketing
definitions, 1, 2

216